THE BEDFORD SERIES IN HISTORY AND CULTURE

Discourse on the Origin and Foundations of Inequality among Men

by Jean-Jacques Rousseau

WITH RELATED DOCUMENTS

THE BEDFORD SERIES IN HISTORY AND CULTURE

Discourse on the Origin and Foundations of Inequality among Men

by Jean-Jacques Rousseau

WITH RELATED DOCUMENTS

Translated, Edited, and with an Introduction by

Helena Rosenblatt

The Graduate Center of the City University of New York

BEDFORD / ST. MARTIN'S　　　Boston ◆ New York

For Bedford/St. Martin's

Publisher for History: Mary V. Dougherty
Director of Development for History: Jane Knetzger
Senior Editor: Heidi L. Hood
Developmental Editor: Shannon Hunt
Editorial Assistant: Jennifer Jovin
Production Associate: Ashley Chalmers
Executive Marketing Manager: Jenna Bookin Barry
Project Management: Books By Design, Inc.
Index: Books By Design, Inc.
Text Design: Claire Seng-Niemoeller
Cover Design: Donna L. Dennison
Cover Art: *Portrait of Jean-Jacques Rousseau* (1712–1778) (pastel on paper) by Maurice
   Quentin de la Tour (1704–1788). Musée Antoine Lecuyer, Saint-Quentin, France/
   Giraudon/The Bridgeman Art Library.
Composition: Achorn International
Printing and Binding: RR Donnelley & Sons Company

President: Joan E. Feinberg
Editorial Director: Denise B. Wydra
Director of Marketing: Karen R. Soeltz
Director of Production: Susan W. Brown
Associate Director of Editorial Production: Elise S. Kaiser
Manager, Publishing Services: Emily Berleth

Library of Congress Control Number: 2010928028

Manufactured in the United States of America.

5 4 3 2 1 0
f e d c b a

For information, write: Bedford/St. Martin's, 75 Arlington Street, Boston, MA 02116
(617-399-4000)

ISBN-10: 0-312-46842-3
ISBN-13: 978-0-312-46842-2

Acknowledgments

Acknowledgments and copyrights appear at the back of the book on page 156, which
constitutes an extension of the copyright page.

Foreword

The Bedford Series in History and Culture is designed so that readers can study the past as historians do. The historian's first task is finding the evidence. Documents, letters, memoirs, interviews, pictures, movies, novels, or poems can provide facts and clues. Then the historian questions and compares the sources. There is more to do than in a courtroom, for hearsay evidence is welcome, and the historian is usually looking for answers beyond act and motive. Different views of an event may be as important as a single verdict. How a story is told may yield as much information as what it says. Along the way the historian seeks help from other historians and perhaps from specialists in other disciplines. Finally, it is time to write, to decide on an interpretation and how to arrange the evidence for readers.

Each book in this series contains an important historical document or group of documents, each document a witness from the past and open to interpretation in different ways. The documents are combined with some element of historical narrative—an introduction or a biographical essay, for example—that provides students with an analysis of the primary source material and important background information about the world in which it was produced.

Each book in the series focuses on a specific topic within a specific historical period. Each provides a basis for lively thought and discussion about several aspects of the topic and the historian's role. Each is short enough (and inexpensive enough) to be a reasonable one-week assignment in a college course. Whether as classroom or personal reading, each book in the series provides firsthand experience of the challenge—and fun—of discovering, recreating, and interpreting the past.

Lynn Hunt
David W. Blight
Bonnie G. Smith
Natalie Zemon Davis
Ernest R. May

v

Preface

This volume is dedicated to one of the most important texts in the Western political tradition: *Discourse on the Origin and Foundations of Inequality among Men*, by Jean-Jacques Rousseau, which is also known as the Second Discourse. In response to an essay question posed by the Academy of Dijon, Rousseau launched an assault upon the supposedly God-given social hierarchy of the time and questioned the superiority of civilized society. His work provoked the ire of fellow Enlightenment *philosophes* and alienated him from the intellectual world of Paris, yet later democratic and socialist leaders seized upon his assertions and elevated him as a champion of the people. Although Rousseau's ideas were all but dismissed during his lifetime, they ultimately transformed political thinking and helped inspire revolutions.

The Second Discourse will introduce students to Rousseau's radical perspective on concepts such as the state of nature, the social contract, and the general will, which have been essential to the development of modern democratic thought. Students will also encounter Rousseau's devastating critique of private property, which anticipated communism, and his attack on the values of modern "civilization," which is as thought-provoking today as it was in the eighteenth century. They will have the opportunity to grapple with the profound and timeless questions Rousseau raised: Who are we, and where do we come from? What does it mean to be a human being? Why is our society organized the way it is? Could and should it be organized differently? An accessible introduction describes Rousseau's background and life story in a way that illuminates his intellectual development and highlights some of his most radical and innovative ideas. In addition to examining Rousseau's political and moral thoughts, the introduction also addresses his scientific views, such as his perspectives on human evolution and gender, and the reaction to his later works.

Included in this volume are important related documents, including key excerpts from Rousseau's other masterpiece, *The Social Contract*, which gives students a broader picture of his often paradoxical views. Other selections allow students to compare Rousseau with various great political thinkers. They include excerpts from Jacques-Bénigne Bossuet, the divine-right theorist; Thomas Hobbes and Samuel von Pufendorf, two absolute monarchists; John Locke, the constitutional monarchist; and Benjamin Constant, the early-nineteenth-century liberal. Brief selections from George-Louis Leclerc de Buffon, the eighteenth-century scientist, and Maximilien Robespierre, the French revolutionary, are included to remind us of the scientific context in which Rousseau wrote and the political uses to which his ideas could be put. Each document is accompanied by an explanatory headnote that provides historical context as well as biographical information about the author.

At the end of the volume, instructors will find a chronology of the main events in Rousseau's life, a list of questions suitable for discussion or for writing assignments, and a selected bibliography with suggestions for further reading.

ACKNOWLEDGMENTS

I would like to thank Lynn Hunt, who invited me to undertake this project, and also Mary Dougherty, Jane Knetzger, Heidi Hood, and Jennifer Jovin, who helped guide me through it. I am indebted to Shannon Hunt, developmental editor, who has been immensely helpful and pleasant to work with, and Nancy Benjamin for her meticulous care with the proofs. I am also grateful to those reviewers who read and commented on my first draft: Gregory Brown, University of Nevada, Las Vegas; Marybeth Carlson, University of Dayton; Patrick Coleman, University of California, Los Angeles; William Olejniczak, College of Charleston; Timothy Schroer, University of West Georgia; Charlie R. Steen, University of New Mexico; and K. Steven Vincent, State University of North Carolina at Raleigh. Finally I would like to thank Paul Schweigert, a student at the Graduate Center, CUNY, for his feedback on my introduction.

Helena Rosenblatt

A Note about the Text and Translation

This translation is based on the Pléiade edition of Rousseau's *Oeuvres complètes* (vol. III, pp. 109–223), published in 1964 and considered the standard. However, I have also used the Heinrich Meier edition, which contains some important corrections. I have consulted, and learned much from, the translations and annotations of Julia Conaway Bondanella, Donald Cress, Victor Gourevitch, and Roger and Judith Masters, and I acknowledge my indebtedness to them here.

In my own translation, I have tried to stay as close to Rousseau's words and phrasing as possible. This is why I have left a few words or concepts in the original French. They are *amour de soi-même*, *amour propre*, and *mœurs*. Although *amour de soi-même* translates directly to "self-love," there is no English equivalent for *amour propre*. As Rousseau explains in Note XV, *amour propre* is a "relative" and "artificial" sentiment, "born in society." It is a socialized form of *amour de soi-même*. Although *amour propre* is sometimes translated as "vanity" in other English-language editions, Rousseau makes it quite clear that vanity is only one type of *amour propre*. For this reason, and in order to respect Rousseau's desire to contrast the two similar-sounding terms, I have left them in French. Neither is there a modern-day English equivalent for the eighteenth-century French word *mœurs*. To translate it as either "manners" or "morals," as is often done, is to distort the meaning. The word refers to both manners and morals simultaneously—in other words, to beliefs and actions moderated by human customs.

When a second edition of the *Discourse* was published in 1782, Rousseau made a few changes to his text. Those passages appear in bold type. In the related documents, paragraph numbers have been omitted, capitalization has been modernized, and spelling has been Americanized.

Contents

PART ONE

Introduction:
The Life and Thought
of Jean-Jacques Rousseau

Anyone asked to compile a list of the ten or even five most important philosophers in the Western intellectual tradition would almost certainly have to include Jean-Jacques Rousseau (1712–1778). His influence on modern thought has been as broad as it has been deep, mainly because of the extraordinary range of his interests and talents. It would be hard to find another writer who made as many seminal contributions to as many different fields and in as many different genres. At various points in his life he distinguished himself as an essayist, composer, novelist, memoirist, and botanist.

But Rousseau's greatest and most enduring impact is undoubtedly as a moral and political thinker. It is as the author of the *Discourse on the Origin and Foundations of Inequality among Men* (1755) that he became known as a pioneer of modern individualism on the one hand and the spiritual father of socialism on the other. It is this text, along with his *Social Contract* (1762), that earned Rousseau a reputation for being the most egalitarian and democratic of all political theorists and a tireless champion of the poor, the downtrodden, and the oppressed. It is also in this essay that Rousseau delivered one of the most famous and enduring critiques of modern civilization.

Commonly referred to as the Second Discourse, it is probably Rousseau's most creative and radical work, and broadest in its range of

1

influence. Not only did it shatter the reigning political ideologies of his time, but it contained seminal contributions to fields in the natural sciences that were just beginning to emerge, such as linguistics, anthropology, sociology, and psychology. His work also anticipated the development of fields like evolutionary biology.

An extremely provocative text, the Second Discourse has always triggered strong reactions in readers. Since it first appeared more than 250 years ago, people have responded with emotions ranging from shock and outrage to fascination and quasi-religious reverence. Today, it continues to prod people to think—and to think deeply—about issues of perennial importance in both politics and the sciences.

ROUSSEAU'S BEGINNINGS: THE ROAD TO THE SECOND DISCOURSE

Jean-Jacques Rousseau was born in Geneva on June 28, 1712, to Isaac Rousseau, a watchmaker and citizen of that city, and Suzanne Bernard Rousseau, his beautiful and much adored wife. Suzanne's family was wealthy and well connected, and thanks to her, the Rousseau family first lived in the elegant section of town.

During the Protestant Reformation, Geneva had renounced the Catholic Church and had embraced the theology and strict code of conduct advanced by John Calvin (1509–1564), a French exile in that city. At the time of Rousseau's birth, Geneva was an independent and Calvinist republic, and being a citizen of the city conferred substantial political rights and privileges. In contrast to France, which was ruled by a king who claimed absolute political authority, Geneva's ancient constitution was democratic.[1] Being Genevan was therefore a source of pride to men like Isaac Rousseau, who conveyed his republican and patriotic sentiments to his son. The religious and the political culture of Geneva left a lasting imprint on the young Jean-Jacques.

Very early in his life, however, Rousseau suffered a series of devastating losses that forged in him an acute sense of social and political injustice. His mother died nine days after his birth. Later his father ran into financial difficulties, forcing the family to move to the poorer section of town. Finally, Isaac Rousseau ran afoul of the law in a political squabble: After an altercation with a man who had political connections, Isaac was forced to leave the city at once or face jail. One can only imagine the effects these events would have had on his highly intelligent, and highly sensitive, young son.

Rendered a virtual orphan at the age of ten, Jean-Jacques was now consigned to his maternal uncle, who appears to have offered little in the way of parental affection or guidance. He was placed in the home of a country pastor, where he was reasonably happy. After two years his uncle tried to find him suitable employment, but twice these efforts failed. He was fired from his first job as a legal clerk on the grounds of "incompetence"[2] and soon became miserable in his second job as an apprentice engraver. It was not so much the work that disturbed him as it was his master's tyrannical and abusive behavior. Reduced to stealing food to quell his hunger, he was beaten regularly when his master found out.

Rousseau's unhappiness helps to explain an impulsive decision he made one Sunday evening in March 1728. He had acquired the habit of taking walks outside the city gates on Sunday afternoons. On that particular Sunday evening, he found the gates closed when he returned a bit late. Twice this had happened before and, each time, he had been punished severely by his master the following morning. This time, Rousseau chose to leave Geneva for good. He was only sixteen.

Penniless and without any connections, he wandered around the Genevan countryside for a few days, relying upon the hospitality of strangers. In an act of youthful rebellion, or perhaps out of enlightened self-interest, he converted to Catholicism at the behest of a sympathetic priest. The fact that he thereby forfeited his rights to Genevan citizenship did not deter him. He then led a vagabond life for several years, spending time in and around the provincial towns of Annecy, Chambéry, and Lyons. Forced to live on charity, or on the meager earnings provided by the occasional odd job, he suffered the frustrations and humiliations of being poor.

Eventually, in search of fame and fortune, Rousseau made his way to Paris. When he arrived in 1742, at the age of thirty, Paris was the dominant cultural force in Europe. Moreover, it was the capital of the Enlightenment, an exciting intellectual movement that promoted critical thinking and reform. On the cutting edge of this movement were the *philosophes*, a French term for the thinkers who wished to open people's minds, change the way they thought, and thereby improve society.

Despite his poverty and provincial background, Rousseau encountered early success in Paris. He gravitated to, and was accepted by, the *philosophes*. He frequented the fashionable salons and cafés where the latest, most progressive ideas were being discussed. He met and befriended Denis Diderot and got to know other progressive intellectuals, like Étienne Bonnot de Condillac; Friedrich Melchior, Baron von Grimm; and Jean le Rond d'Alembert.

But these continued to be difficult times for Rousseau. He was still poor and, like other struggling intellectuals, was constantly obliged to find work or wealthy patrons. He found the jobs he was forced to take degrading and the system that provided them exploitative and unfair. In his *Confessions*, an autobiography that he wrote much later in life, he remembered that all of these experiences had politicized him. A year spent as the secretary to the French ambassador in Venice had left in his mind a "germ of indignation against our stupid civil institutions in which real public good and real justice are always sacrificed." His voracious reading during this period helped him to arrive at an important conclusion: "Everything depended on politics."[3] When he returned to Paris, all he could see around him was "the oppression of the weak and the iniquity of the strong."[4]

The years from 1744 to 1749 were especially difficult. Having to struggle against poverty in the midst of so much opulence made Rousseau feel "disgusted with society." In texts written around this time, he described Paris as a "town where arrogance rules and where the virtuous poor are the object of contempt."[5] In France's capital city, learned men were being turned into "base parasites," forced to sell their witticisms for a meal.[6]

During these hard times, Rousseau took comfort in his growing friendship with Diderot. The two men had much in common. Both were sons of craftsmen, both were from the provinces, and both were brilliant, yet struggling, *philosophes*. In 1747, Diderot began editing what would eventually become a crowning achievement of the French Enlightenment: the twenty-eight-volume *Encyclopedia, or Reasoned Dictionary of the Sciences, Arts and Trades*. Toward the end of 1748, he asked Rousseau to collaborate with him on this project. Rousseau would contribute many articles on music and one on political economy.

No wonder, then, that Rousseau was struck particularly hard when his friend was suddenly arrested and thrown in jail. Without warning, trial, or hearing, royal agents appeared on Diderot's doorstep one morning in July 1749 and hauled him off to the fortress of Vincennes, where he was placed in solitary confinement. Diderot was arrested because some of his writings had offended the authorities. More specifically, his *Letter on the Blind* had questioned arguments traditionally made to prove the existence of God. Rousseau later described his emotional distress when he heard the news: "I nearly went out of my mind."[7]

Due to the intercession of friends, Diderot was eventually allowed to receive visitors, and Rousseau began making regular trips to Vincennes. Each time, he traveled the six miles by foot. On one of those long walks, he had a life-altering experience. He had brought along a copy of *Le Mercure de France*, a popular literary magazine. Pausing a moment to read it under a tree, he came across the announcement of an essay competition sponsored by the Academy of Dijon. The question posed was "Has the Restoration of the Sciences and the Arts Contributed to the Purification of Morals?" Years later, Rousseau remembered the emotions and ideas that suddenly welled up inside him as he read those words. He experienced an "illumination": "I beheld another universe and became another man."[8]

Today, the essay question posed by the Dijon Academy sounds fairly innocuous. It seems that contestants were being asked to consider whether the arts and sciences improve us morally. At the time, however, the question was a sensitive one politically. In essence, it invited people to evaluate the merits of the Enlightenment, a movement that many people worried was subversive of tradition. Diderot's imprisonment for authoring "dangerous" texts exemplified this fear.

Under the circumstances, one might have expected Rousseau to jump at the chance to defend the Enlightenment. After all, he was an aspiring *philosophe* himself. Instead, he did something very different and thereby launched his career as an intellectual provocateur. His *Discourse on the Sciences and Arts* attacked the Enlightenment head-on. He accused the movement of being frivolous, vain, and self-serving. Not only was the Enlightenment *not* promoting moral progress, Rousseau wrote, it was fostering the very opposite: moral and political corruption.

The essay, now known as the First Discourse, won first prize; and overnight, Rousseau became a celebrity. Many people were delighted and amused by his essay. They admired his writing style and thought the piece a kind of clever joke. Others were confused and angered. Nobody thought that Rousseau was serious. How could a contributor to the *Encyclopedia* deny the value of the arts and sciences? How could a *philosophe* attack the Enlightenment? Voltaire, the most famous *philosophe* of all, was outraged. At the time the essay appeared, he was living in Berlin, in the entourage of his patron, Frederick the Great. Voltaire wrote contemptuously, "I am hardly in a position, at the court of the King of Prussia, to read themes composed by school boys for prizes offered by the academy of Dijon."[9]

Having not yet read Rousseau's discourse, Voltaire probably did not realize how ironic his words were, since the essay contained a political message pointed directly at him. In essence, Rousseau accused the *philosophes* of flattering the rich and powerful and of thereby becoming the props of unjust and corrupt regimes. He singled out Voltaire for special rebuke. Addressing him as the "Famed Arouet" (Arouet being Voltaire's real name), Rousseau accused Voltaire of being more interested in his own fame than in anything truly worthwhile. In carefully chosen words and only slightly veiled allusions, Rousseau urged the *philosophes* to become more political. The recent intellectual revival, he wrote, only spread "garlands of flowers over the chains with which [men are] burdened."[10] In one remarkable passage, Rousseau warned people that governments were only too glad to use the arts and sciences for their own sinister purposes:

> Princes always view with pleasure the dissemination, among their subjects, of a taste for the agreeable Arts. . . . For, in addition to fostering in them that pettiness of soul so appropriate to servitude, they know well that all the needs that a People imposes on itself are so many chains that burden it.[11]

Rousseau's First Discourse launched a debate that would rage for more than a year. Many people responded by defending the Enlightenment, learning in general, and the arts and sciences in particular. Rousseau was accused of being a hypocrite, a scoundrel, an irresponsible provocateur. When he went on to publish a play (*Narcissus*) and then composed a very popular opera (*The Village Soothsayer*), which was performed before the King himself, it only added to the controversy swirling around him. How could a man attack the arts and contribute to them at the same time?

Prompted by the criticism, Rousseau wrote several replies. He refused to back down. Instead, he began to refine his thoughts and deepen his analysis of what he increasingly saw as the political and social sources of society's corruption. Simultaneously, Rousseau tried to reform himself, so that he might live according to his principles. He withdrew from fashionable society. He refused all gifts and patronage, choosing to earn a modest income as a music copyist. He became more and more estranged from his *philosophe* friends.

Then, in the fall of 1753, the Dijon Academy announced another essay competition. This time, the question posed was "What is the origin of inequality among men, and is it authorized by natural law?" Rousseau later recounted that he was "struck by that great question, and surprised that the Academy had dared to propose it." He seized the opportunity to develop his principles "more fully" than he had until then.[12] The result was the *Discourse on the Origin and Foundations of Inequality among Men*.

In it, Rousseau delivered a devastating critique of the reigning social and political system. Having merely criticized society for being vain and self-satisfied in the First Discourse, he now shocked everyone with a blistering attack on society's very foundations. He identified economic and political inequality as the root of all evil and singled out the institution of private property for special condemnation. He broadcast clearly, for the first time, what would become the animating principle of his life's work: the idea that man, although born good, was corrupted by his institutions. Rousseau began his argument by distinguishing between two kinds of inequality: "physical" and "moral." By "physical" inequality, he meant inborn powers of the body or mind. Some people are born stronger than others; some people are born cleverer than others. Such disparities were of little importance to Rousseau. They were simply a fact of life that one had to accept. "Moral inequality," however, was a different matter. It referred to the principle that some people have more authority or power than others. By making this distinction, Rousseau was able to transform a question about the origin of inequality into a question about the origin of political authority. He could then condemn both inequality and the modern governments that legitimized it. At the end of his essay, he predicted that such governments would end in revolution.

THE ORIGINS OF POLITICAL AUTHORITY

In eighteenth-century France, there existed two main schools of thought on the origins of government: the theory of the divine right of kings and that of the social contract. The French monarchy based its legitimacy on the former. Kings were placed on their thrones by God. The theory had medieval roots but had been refined over the course of the seventeenth century. In France, its chief exponent was Jacques-Bénigne Bossuet (1627–1704). Basing his political principles directly on the Bible and on theological notions like original sin, Bossuet argued that the king's authority was both absolute and sacred (Document 1). Although he was supposed to use his power to further the public good, the king was accountable for his actions to God alone. Those who questioned the king's power threatened to plunge society into chaos and disorder. They were also rebels against the will of God, as law-abiding Christians were required to submit to the God-given social and political order.

By the middle of the eighteenth century, the theory of the divine right of kings had been under attack for some time. Many people rejected orthodox notions of original sin and the idea that God appointed kings. Since the seventeenth century, theorists belonging to the so-called school of natural law, such as Hugo Grotius (1583–1645) and Samuel von Pufendorf (1632–1694), and major political thinkers, such as Thomas Hobbes (1588–1679) and John Locke (1632–1704), had developed secular explanations for the origins of governments. They argued that governments were the result of a contract negotiated between free and equal individuals. During the Enlightenment, such theories were widely disseminated through the publications of Jean Barbeyrac (1674–1744) and Jean-Jacques Burlamaqui (1694–1748). The *Encyclopedia* also did much to popularize them. Its articles "Political Authority" and "Government" state unequivocally that the true source of political authority is the consent of the people.

Note that the belief in social contract theory did not make its advocates egalitarian. Instead, their ideas actually justified various forms of *in*equality. Grotius, Pufendorf, and Hobbes constructed theories that legitimized absolute monarchy. Locke, Barbeyrac, and Burlamaqui preferred more liberal types of government; however, they too were prepared to accept a considerable amount of social, economic, and political inequality in society. None advocated democracy, which Burlamaqui described as "the weakest and perhaps the worst of governments."[13] In fact, on the issue of inequality, social contract and divine right of kings theorists were in substantial agreement: While individuals had been "naturally equal" in the state of nature, they could no longer be equal in society.

On this issue, the French *philosophes* essentially concurred. In some vague, abstract sense, men were naturally equal. They had the same basic needs and entered society for the same reasons. But the *philosophes* also knew, and accepted, that in society, men were unequal. Some people were rich, and others were poor; some people led, and others followed. The *philosophes* regarded this situation as natural, inevitable, and necessary for the smooth functioning of society. They often argued that such differences were useful, since they caused interdependence, binding people together through their mutual needs.

The article "Society" in the *Encyclopedia* is a case in point. It states that natural equality is a principle that "should never be lost from sight." But it then goes on to claim that "differences of condition" and even subordination are necessary for the sake of happiness and order. According to "the contract," individuals who live in society have agreed that "some are above, others are below." Without such inequalities, society would only devolve into "confusion, trouble, [and] dissension."[14]

To explain the origins of government, social contract theorists imagined what life would be like without any political authority. They called this condition the "state of nature." They described it as a state in which each individual enjoyed perfect freedom and equality. They then imagined what might have led individuals to leave this state of nature to form a society under a government.

Early contract theorists tended to have a dark view of human nature. One of the most famous among them, Thomas Hobbes, believed that men were naturally driven by violent and destructive passions (Document 2). Samuel von Pufendorf disagreed with some of Hobbes's details but similarly stressed man's "natural malice." He added that man was naturally weak and helpless, needing the assistance of others (Document 3). Such negative portrayals of man in the state of nature helped Hobbes and Pufendorf explain why people would give up their natural liberty and equality and submit to a strong government.

John Locke, however, had a more positive view of human nature. He described men in the state of nature as being endowed with reason. Their reason meant that they could apprehend moral laws, such as the injunction not to hurt one another. Nevertheless, Locke also referred to "Confusion and Disorder" arising in the state of nature. Various "Inconveniences"[15] there led men to set up governments.

Well versed in social contract theory, French *philosophes* did not spend much time pondering why men would want to leave the state of nature. It was obvious to them that they would prefer all the advantages of life in society. Under the protection of wise governments and good laws, they could enjoy the peace and order necessary for their survival and happiness.

In the eighteenth century, the idea that man was "naturally sociable" gained currency, eventually becoming a key concept for the *philosophes*.[16] "Natural sociability" referred to a whole cluster of ideas. Pufendorf had written that naturally weak and needy individuals had a selfish interest in procuring the help of others. To him, this meant that sociability was a "fundamental natural law."[17] Locke had written more optimistically that men were "naturally induced to seek communion and fellowship with others."[18] Following Lockean reasoning, the *Encyclopedia* claimed that men were naturally disposed to feel goodwill toward other human beings. Such sentiments of sociability were both a "natural penchant" and a gift from God. Everyone agreed that sociability drew people together and caused them to cooperate with one another for the benefit of all. To the *philosophes*, it was clear proof that "men were made to live in society."[19]

ROUSSEAU'S BOMBSHELL: THE *DISCOURSE ON THE ORIGIN AND FOUNDATIONS OF INEQUALITY AMONG MEN*

By 1753, when Rousseau read the Dijon Academy's essay question, he no longer agreed with such optimistic ways of thinking. To him, society was *not* organized so as to promote everyone's happiness and welfare. The question invited him to evaluate the ideas of the school of natural law and their theories of social contract. He could see many holes and contradictions in their arguments. Why on earth would originally free and equal individuals agree to a contract that legitimized gross economic and political inequalities? Why would they consent to their own subjugation? His answer was startling: The majority of mankind must have been tricked. Established governments, and the inequalities that they enforced, were the result of a giant hoax perpetrated by the rich on the poor.

Rousseau's description of the state of nature was designed to counter the arguments of his predecessors. He refuted the social contract theorists' descriptions of man in the state of nature and their reasons for why man entered society. Against Hobbes, Rousseau argued that there was no reason to suppose that natural man should be fearful, angry, and violent. Against Pufendorf, he argued that there was also no reason to think that he should be weak and need others for his survival. The social contract theorists' mistake had been to transport to the state of nature ideas, passions, and needs that man could only have acquired in society.

In Part One, Rousseau thus stripped man of all the accretions he thought he had acquired from living in society. Rousseau's natural man was both strong and gentle. A solitary creature, he had none of the passions that plagued civilized man. Living alone among the animals, he was very much like them. Self-sufficient and at peace with his environment, he was neither sociable nor unsociable, neither moral nor immoral.

Having challenged the social contract theorists' assumptions about the state of nature, Rousseau also challenged their conclusions. There was no natural need for men to leave the state of nature and to submit to government. In fact, man might have lived forever in the state of nature if a series of "fatal accidents" had not intervened.

The Steps to Society

According to Rousseau, it was external circumstances, rather than any "natural sociability," or any pressing needs, that caused men to leave the state of nature. In Part Two of the Second Discourse, he described what he thought must have been the very long and drawn-out process of man's gradual departure from the state of nature. He recounted it as a series of stages in man's slow socialization. In so doing, Rousseau transformed the social contract theorists' state of nature into something quite different. For Hobbes and Pufendorf, the state of nature was a theoretical construct. Neither one suggested that any human being had actually lived in the state of nature. In fact, Rousseau also claimed to be offering only speculations about a state "that perhaps never existed" (p. 37). Nevertheless, he described it much more like an actual period in human history. He included an unprecedented amount of environmental and biological detail in order to bring this period, and its successive stages, to life.

What made men leave the state of nature? Rousseau began by considering the challenges that probably arose within that state. Nature presented obstacles that men were forced to overcome, and new situations to which they were obliged to adapt. As the population grew, it spread, and the difficulties multiplied. A scarcity of food obliged men to discover new ways to subsist. They learned to fish and hunt.

As men became more numerous, they began to encounter one another more frequently. In the course of these random encounters, they started to perceive the advantages that might come from occasionally cooperating with one another, such as, for example, when hunting a large animal. Slowly, men in the state of nature began to alter their behavior and lifestyle accordingly.

Chance occurrences also played a role in transforming men's lives. Rousseau suggests that a "happy accident" (p. 71), like a bolt of lightning or a volcano, probably taught men fire. Other accidents caused them to discover that they could use stones as tools. They learned to employ them to dig the earth and to build huts in which to live.

Once men had huts, a new lifestyle became possible. Rousseau refers to this as a "first revolution" (p. 73) in the state of nature. Men became more sedentary, and family life became possible. Many pleasures were invented that made life more comfortable. For Rousseau, this hut stage was a kind of golden age for mankind—a middle stage of human development. While there was some social life, there was not yet any government. While there was a kind of property, there was not yet the modern type. Nor was there any real division of labor. Everyone carried out the same simple tasks and occasionally collaborated on communal ones. Men lived "free, healthy, good, and happy" (p. 76). Rousseau reasoned that only another accident could have made man leave the hut stage. This time it was a fatal and not a happy one: the discovery of metallurgy and agriculture. From this development came the division of labor, the partition of land, and most important, the invention of property. Once property was invented, a social contract became necessary, and civil society was formed.

Two aspects of this story merit special attention here. First, Rousseau's account identifies him as one of the first to sketch a theory of socioeconomic evolution.[20] In essence, what he describes are successive stages of human development, each one depending on a different mode of subsistence. Man starts out as a gatherer, becomes a hunter, and then turns into a farmer, before finally entering into a modern society based on industry and trade. His changing means of subsistence propel the story forward.

Second, Rousseau's repeated reference to accidents is interesting. It implies that history need not have happened the way it did. In other words, neither "God" nor "providence" nor "nature" dictated the course of human history. Therefore, neither God nor providence nor nature would necessarily sanction the present socioeconomic and political order. This was an unsettling claim to make in eighteenth-century France, and it added to the revolutionary flavor of Rousseau's essay. He suggested that the established order was largely based on accidents and mistakes made by man.

The Invention of Property

Rousseau's attack on property has always been regarded as an especially provocative and innovative part of the Second Discourse. His fellow *philosophes* tended to view property as an unquestionable right, sanctioned by both nature and reason. They rarely gave much thought to the origins of property and simply took it for granted that it was the government's role to protect it. On this, they could rely on the authority of John Locke (Document 4). In his *Second Treatise of Government*, Locke explained how man in the state of nature acquired property and thereafter formed societies to protect it. Several articles in the *Encyclopedia* followed Locke's basic reasoning, stating as a matter of fact that men left the state of nature to "assure their possessions" and that the purpose of governments was to "protect their property."[21]

In the Second Discourse, Rousseau did not deny Locke's idea of how property arose in the state of nature; nor did he refute the idea that a social contract eventually became necessary to protect property. What he did, rather, was to deny the legitimacy of these things. He described property's invention as a tragic moment in history, and one that might have been avoided if only people had had more foresight. Thereafter, differences in strength and talents led to differences in wealth and power, and the equality of the state of nature was destroyed. Property—and the inequality that resulted from it—led to crime, general disorder, warfare, and unhappiness.

Rousseau then postulated that it must have been the rich who thought up the idea of the social contract. Essentially, they tricked the poor into believing that the social contract would protect everyone. They hoodwinked them into giving up their liberty, "the most noble of man's faculties" (p. 86). Tragically, then, people unwittingly submitted to an unjust and dehumanizing system based on the exploitation of the poor and the dominance of the rich.

The situation seems utterly hopeless, unless one pays heed to Rousseau's statement that it is equivalent to a new state of nature. He further explains that under the circumstances, "the contract of government is . . . completely dissolved" (p. 93). Perhaps it is time for a new social contract, one that should be negotiated on different grounds.

Anthropology, Psychology, and Evolutionary Biology

While Rousseau's account of man's socioeconomic and political history was innovative and provocative, so was his description of the transformations that human nature had undergone over the course of that history. At the outset of the Second Discourse, he calls attention to the "changes that the succession of time and things must have produced in [man's] original constitution" (p. 36). He then tracks these changes, both physical and mental, in the rest of the essay. The attention paid to human nature's evolution made the Second Discourse a pioneering text in the fields of anthropology, psychology, and evolutionary biology.

Most people at the time believed in the immutability of the human species: They assumed that the human beings of one period in history were the same as the human beings of another. Moreover, most people still relied on the Bible as a historical record of early human history. Rousseau, however, vowed at the outset of the Second Discourse not to use any "supernatural knowledge." Instead, he would rely on information culled from books of natural science, such as George-Louis Leclerc de Buffon's *Natural History* (Document 5), and from the descriptions of savages found in books like Antoine-François Prévost's *Histoire générale des voyages.*[22] With this, presumably more reliable, data, Rousseau postulated that human nature was not static, but had evolved over time. One hundred years before Charles Darwin, Rousseau speculated that both our mental capacities and our physical characteristics had changed in response to changes in our environment. In one of his important notes appended to the Second Discourse, he even suggested that modern Europeans might be descended from the large apes described by travelers to the Congo (pp. 110–13).

Natural scientists in the eighteenth century often compared human beings to animals. Such comparisons were used to support their notions about man's superiority on the Great Chain of Being that linked all of God's creation.[23] Some people pointed to man's soul; others referred to his rational mind. Man's ability to speak was also regarded as a defining feature of his humanity. In the Second Discourse, Rousseau adopted the comparative method of the natural scientists, but he rejected many of their assumptions and conclusions. Mainly, he was willing to "animalize" man to a greater extent than they. He speculated that our primitive ancestors had probably not been more rational than the orangutans presently found in Africa; nor was it likely that early humans had been any better at verbal communication. Rousseau imagined that both reason and speech were only "potential faculties" in natural man and had required centuries of evolution and development in order to emerge.[24]

What distinguished man from the animals in Rousseau's estimation was neither his rationality nor his capacity to speak. Rather, it was his free will, or what Rousseau described as man's unique capacity to act as a free agent and to choose or will what he wished. Then there was also man's "perfectibility" (p. 52), a word coined by Rousseau, and by which he meant man's ability to adapt to circumstances and to evolve over time. Rousseau went on to recount how the various accidents that had changed man's means of subsistence had also changed his physical and psychological nature. "Circumstances" had brought forth his ability to reflect, to speak, to experience emotions, and to perceive moral laws.

Perhaps especially noteworthy is Rousseau's account of the emergence of man's social passions. Man in the pure state of nature was moved only by a concern for his own survival, tempered by an ability to feel pity for others. Living a solitary existence, he felt none of the "relative" passions that plague modern man, like pride, vanity, greed, and jealousy. Such passions only emerged over time, as men interacted

Figure 1. During the mid-eighteenth century, there was much discussion about what it is that separates human beings from apes. This image of a very human-looking "jocko," or chimpanzee, appeared in George-Louis Leclerc de Buffon's famous *Natural History* (Document 5), a book that Rousseau cites repeatedly in his notes.

From George-Louis Leclerc de Buffon, *Histoire générale et particulière, avec la description du cabinet du roi* (Paris: De l'Imprimerie Royale, 1749–1804). Wellcome Library, London.

socially. Occasional contact with other human beings brought forth the capacity to reflect and make comparisons. This triggered "the first stirring of pride" (p. 71). More sustained contact with others led to the birth of vanity. A settled, domesticated existence awakened positive and pleasant emotions like love, as well as negative and hurtful ones like jealousy. The invention of property gave birth to competitiveness and greed. Equally noteworthy is Rousseau's contention that morals are socially generated. There was no moral law, such as Locke had proposed, inscribed by God on the hearts of men in the state of nature. Incapable even of reflection, primitive man could not have known moral rules. Like our "relative" passions, our ideas of right and wrong came into existence over time and in the course of our socialization.

Rousseau and Gender

Because of what he wrote in other texts, mainly the *Letter to d'Alembert*; *Julie, or the New Heloise*; and *Emile*, Rousseau has acquired the reputation of being a confirmed sexist, if not a misogynist. In these other writings, women are repeatedly made to play cloistered, domestic, and subordinate roles. This has led many readers to conclude that Rousseau himself believed in a strict gender hierarchy and in separate spheres for men and women. In support of this argument, one could also point to the Dedication of the Second Discourse, in which Rousseau praises Genevan women for sex-specific virtues and for playing essentially supportive roles within the patriarchal family.

In the main text of the Second Discourse, however, a very different picture emerges. Here Rousseau describes women as naturally strong, independent, and free. In his version of the state of nature, women are the equals of men, and the family does not even exist. Such ideas contrast markedly with those found in the writings of other social contract theorists.[25] According to Pufendorf, for example, it was obvious that man enjoyed "superior[ity]" over woman in the state of nature.[26] Similarly, in Locke's rendition, the husband was clearly "the abler and stronger" person.[27] Then there was, of course, the biblical pronouncement: God ordained Adam to rule over his wife as punishment for original sin.[28] In contrast, Rousseau suggests that families are only social conventions. His description of women thus reinforces the larger message of the Second Discourse: Much of what we think is natural is actually artificial;

our social arrangements are the product of habits acquired over time. This applies to gender roles as well. They are *constructed*, not natural.

Reception of the Second Discourse

With this competition entry, Rousseau did not win a prize. Annoyed by his essay's length and content, the jury did not even bother to finish reading it. Instead they awarded first prize to an entry that defended political and economic inequalities as natural, legitimate, and approved by God. Its author regarded such inequalities as a just punishment for original sin.[29] Second place was given to a law student who argued virtually the same thing. Even extreme economic inequalities were proof of God's "wisdom" and "equity."[30] The French king's absolute authority was similarly praised as being just and willed by providence.

Undeterred by the jury's decision, Rousseau published his essay independently. He was probably disappointed, but not likely surprised, by the reaction it received. Conservatives found it impious and seditious. After all, it began with a denial of original sin and ended in revolution. But Rousseau's *philosophe* friends did not like it either. They found an endless number of contradictions in the essay. Rousseau claimed to be defending human nature; yet he likened human beings to orangutans. He identified "perfectibility" as a distinguishing characteristic of man, and then blamed it for his "decrepitude" (p. 76). He discarded the authority of religion, yet spoke of "the spirituality of [man's] soul" (p. 51). He proposed "setting aside all the facts" (p. 43), and then used an unusual amount of empirical data to support his argument. The list of paradoxes seemed endless.

Most important, however, Rousseau's fellow *philosophes* were taken aback by his excoriation of private property and puzzled by his critique of modernity. They found his ideas "far-fetched" and "ridiculous."[31] When Rousseau sent a copy of his text to Voltaire, that great icon of the Enlightenment responded with characteristic wit and disdain: "I have received, Sir, your new book against humankind; I thank you for it. . . . Never has so much intelligence been used in wanting to make us stupid."[32] In the margins of his text, he scribbled comments like "false," "abominable," and "Here is the philosophy of a beggar who would like to see the rich robbed by the poor."[33] Even one of the most radical *philosophes*, Paul Henri Thiry d'Holbach (1723–1789), urged people to ignore Rousseau's Second Discourse:

Let us not listen to the maxims of a disgruntled and jealous philosopher who, under the pretext of reviving justice . . . would like to annihilate all ranks in order to bring into civil society a chimerical equality that does not even exist among the most savage hordes.[34]

The Second Discourse caused Rousseau's estrangement from the *philosophes* and confirmed his stature as a radical and deeply paradoxical thinker. Once again, people were confused and annoyed. Some thought he had gone mad. The fact that he dedicated the essay to Geneva only added to their dismay.

"Citizen of Geneva": The Dedication

Geneva had never been far from Rousseau's mind since his hasty departure from the city in 1728. Throughout his early years as a vagabond wandering around Europe and the time he spent in Paris as a budding *philosophe*, he was always aware that his Genevan background had shaped his character. He realized that it was one of the reasons he could never "fit in" in Parisian social circles.[35] In 1750, when he attacked French society in his *Discourse on the Sciences and Arts*, he signed his essay "By a Citizen of Geneva" in proud recognition of his republican and Protestant origins.

Technically, however, this signature was false, since Rousseau had officially lost his right to Genevan citizenship when he converted to Catholicism as a teenager. In 1754, he sought to rectify that situation. Prior to publishing the Second Discourse, he returned to Geneva, reconverted to Protestantism, and regained his citizenship. He then wrote the flowery Dedication and appended it to his Discourse.

The Dedication no doubt irritated many people. French readers could take offense at the claim that their values were corrupting. They were probably perplexed by the praise Rousseau heaped on a city that he had, after all, abandoned as a teenager, and by his preference for a "democratic government, wisely tempered" (p. 28). In the eighteenth century, democracy was not considered a viable form of government, especially not in France. Genevans, on the other hand, could take umbrage at the rather heavy-handed lessons the essay contained. As one perceptive Genevan remarked upon reading the piece, "You represent us as we should be, and not as we are."[36] Here again, more than a few readers were taken aback by Rousseau's political views. Mixed in with his effusive praise for Geneva was some stern advice about what real citizenship means and what a just constitution should entail: "The

People" are sovereign, and no one is above the law. Rousseau would elaborate on this democratic vision in *The Social Contract* (1762).

ROUSSEAU'S LATER LIFE AND LEGACY

Rousseau himself considered his Second Discourse a "bold" text and "a work of the greatest importance." He regretted that it "found only a few readers who understood it . . . and [that] none of these wanted to talk about it."[37] Its disappointing reception convinced Rousseau to break with the *philosophes*. He withdrew from society entirely. Preferring solitude to the *philosophes*' much vaunted "sociability," he left Paris and moved into a small secluded house in a forest north of the capital.

This strange behavior only fed the nasty rumors that now circulated about him. How could the self-professed defender of humanity prefer solitude to the company of others? How could he claim to love human beings and yet want to be alone? Did it not prove, once and for all, that he was a hypocrite, perhaps even a "monster," a misanthrope, and an enemy of the human race? In a play published in 1757, Rousseau's former friend Diderot inserted a wounding comment: "Only the bad man lives alone." In 1758, Rousseau responded with *Letter to d'Alembert*, in which he reaffirmed his aversion for much of what the *philosophes* stood for. It sealed his estrangement from them.

But then Rousseau stunned everyone again. In 1761, he published his great sentimental novel, *Julie, or the New Heloise*. It became one of the bestsellers of the eighteenth century. Over forty editions appeared before Rousseau's death, over seventy by the end of the century. So popular was the novel that publishers resorted to renting out chapters by the hour. Overcome by the emotions triggered by the book, thousands of fans wrote letters to Rousseau, expressing their admiration and almost fanatical devotion. It seems that no one before him had ever understood their innermost feelings. Something like a personality cult began to grow around him.

Then, in 1762, disaster struck. Rousseau published two books that the authorities deemed dangerous: *Emile* and *The Social Contract*. Particularly offended by the religious views it contained, Parisian authorities immediately declared *Emile* subversive and issued a warrant for Rousseau's arrest. Alerted in the middle of the night, Rousseau fled to Switzerland. Upon his arrival there, however, he found that the government of Geneva would not provide the refuge he needed. It banned and burned both *Emile* and *The Social Contract* and issued yet another warrant for Rousseau's arrest.

Thus began a painful eight-year period for Rousseau, during which he was a fugitive from justice and lived at the mercy of a few individual protectors. He began to suffer from what appears to have been an emotional crisis. Having already broken with his former friends, he now became obsessed with feelings of persecution and betrayal. He became convinced that they were conspiring against him. In 1764, he publicly renounced his Genevan citizenship.

Rousseau's disturbed psychological state partially explains why he spent many of his final years in deep self-examination. He wrote no fewer than three autobiographies (*Confessions*; *Rousseau, Judge of Jean-Jacques* [also known as the *Dialogues*]; and *Reveries of a Solitary Walker*) in an attempt to understand, and to explain, his troubled relations with the world.[38] Published only after his death, these texts have since become recognized classics.

In 1770, Rousseau was finally allowed to resettle in Paris, but on condition that he refrain from publishing. He led a quiet life, copying music to support himself, studying botany, and working on his autobiographies. He died in 1778.

Rousseau and the French Revolution, 1789–1795

Reviled by some and adored by many, Rousseau had already become a cult figure at the time of his death. During the next decade, this cult grew, fed in part by the publication of his autobiographies and the many revelations they contained. Every part of Rousseau's life was now dissected and discussed. Plays, poems, and essays were written about him. Pilgrimages to his tomb became the fashion. To many people, Rousseau was the very symbol of a good man misunderstood and persecuted by society, and they identified with him.

(Opposite) **Figure 2.** The revolutionaries attached great importance to their central symbols. This *Allegory of the Revolution* (1794), by Nicolas Henri Jeaurat de Bertry, is full of references to key revolutionary concepts like liberty, equality, and fraternity. A portrait of Rousseau is prominently positioned above it all.

An Allegory of the Revolution with a Portrait Medallion of Jean-Jacques Rousseau (1712–1778), 1794 (oil on canvas), Jeaurat de Bertry, Nicolas Henri (1728–1796) / Musée de la Ville de Paris, Musée Carnavalet, Paris, France / The Bridgeman Art Library International.

21

Notably, however, Rousseau's contemporary fame seems to have had little to do with his political works. Scholars debate how much the public even knew of the Second Discourse and *The Social Contract*. Rousseau's reputation had more to do with his novel, *Julie*; his pedagogical book, *Emile*; and his autobiographical *Confessions*.

But the French Revolution changed that. It politicized Rousseau's cult and brought fame to his political ideas. Interestingly, during the first few years of the Revolution, he was quoted on both sides of the political spectrum. Conservatives and counterrevolutionaries noted that he abhorred violence and never wished to cause a revolution. They cited the more pessimistic and skeptical parts of his work. Over time, however, the revolutionaries gained the upper hand and were able to adopt Rousseau as the symbol of their cause. They called him their inspiration, their prophet and guide. They eulogized him in their speeches and honored him with statues and commemorative ceremonies. The most famous revolutionary of all, Maximilien Robespierre, is said to have kept a copy of *The Social Contract* next to his bed. This newly acquired political fame explains that in 1794, sixteen years after Rousseau's death, his remains were ceremoniously transferred to the Panthéon in Paris, where he was buried next to other "national heroes."

In spite of all of this, the exact nature and extent of Rousseau's influence on the revolutionaries continues to be debated. Once again, it is unclear how much of Rousseau's political writings the revolutionaries read and how much of it they understood. There is little evidence that they studied his texts carefully. Moreover, on close inspection, many of Rousseau's political principles seem too abstract to have had practical applications, especially in France.

Nevertheless, the revolutionaries took inspiration from some key Rousseauean ideas. Perhaps most fundamentally, they embraced the notion, first suggested in the Second Discourse, that the past could be repudiated and a new society rebuilt from scratch. They believed that man was naturally good and that if his institutions were corrupt they could be entirely reconceived. Finally, they were inspired by Rousseau's profound egalitarianism, expressed in all of his writings, but perhaps most powerfully in *The Social Contract*.

The Social Contract and Its Paradoxes

Like all of Rousseau's texts, *The Social Contract* (Document 6) has elicited a variety of interpretations. One useful way to read it is as a kind of sequel to the Second Discourse. If the Second Discourse diagnosed a problem, *The Social Contract* proposed a solution. Its purpose was to set out "the principles of political right," in other words, to conceptualize what would constitute a legitimate social contract. The Second Discourse describes the tragic moment in which the poor were tricked into giving up their freedom and submitting to the rule of the rich. Notably, in *The Social Contract*, no such tragic moment occurs. There is no such submission to a person or group of people. Rather, Rousseau's version of the contract seems designed precisely to preserve the freedom and equality of each and every individual while simultaneously uniting them in a political community. In other words, he tried to conceive of a contract that safeguarded everything he thought was moral and good in human beings and that made personal dependence and subjugation impossible. He did this by enlisting the concept of the "general will," a term that Rousseau did not invent but to which he gave new meaning and currency. He linked it provocatively with his notion of "popular sovereignty." It was an explosive combination.

Readers of *The Social Contract* have agreed that Rousseau's vision in it is deeply democratic. Many have also called it problematic. They point to several troubling passages suggesting that the general will should have absolute power over individuals. Paradoxically, then, Rousseau may unwittingly have opened the door to a new and democratic kind of tyranny. Indeed, radicals during the French Revolution invoked key Rousseauean concepts, such as the general will, to justify their despotic powers, supposedly exercised on behalf of "the people."

After the Revolution, those who deplored its most radical and violent aspects often also blamed Rousseau. His name became closely linked with the bloody politics of the Reign of Terror (June 1793–July 1794), when Robespierre was at the height of his power (Document 7). No wonder, then, that liberals of the nineteenth century felt the need to distance themselves from Rousseau's ideas. The more insightful among them, such as Benjamin Constant, attempted to salvage what was good and useful in his thought from what was dangerous or harmful (Document 8). But no great political thinker after Rousseau could afford to ignore him. Much of nineteenth-century political thought was an attempt to come to terms with the French Revolution, and thereby with Rousseau.

In the twentieth century, Rousseau continued to have both admirers and critics, some of whom were fierce. His enemies accused his political philosophy of engendering collectivist tyrannies. He was blamed for the Communist revolutions of the twentieth century and for totalitarianism in general. At the same time, scholarly appreciation for the Second

Discourse grew. Rousseau was increasingly recognized as a founder of modern anthropology and sociology. Today, people continue to debate the meaning of Rousseau's political thought. Was he a democrat, or was he a totalitarian? Was he an individualist, a socialist, a conservative, or an apostle of revolution? Could he have been all of these things? Rousseau's contemporaries called him a "man of paradox" because of the many contradictions they saw in his thought. To this criticism, Rousseau responded:

> Common readers, pardon my paradoxes: They must be made when one thinks seriously; and, whatever you may say, I would rather be a man of paradoxes than a man of prejudices.[39]

In the end, perhaps Rousseau's greatness and longevity as a political thinker are due to his ability to inspire so many different readers and readings. What is certain is that his work continues to speak to us in ways that are both disturbing and enlightening. It provokes deep reflection in anyone who engages with it. Over two hundred years after its first publication, readers are still moved by the problems Rousseau identified, and the principles he expressed, in the *Discourse on the Origin and Foundations of Inequality among Men*.

NOTES

[1] Exactly how democratic it was, and what this actually meant, was the subject of debate in Rousseau's lifetime.

[2] Jean-Jacques Rousseau, *Les Confessions*, in *Œuvres complètes*, ed. Bernard Gagnebin and Marcel Raymond (Paris: Editions Gallimard [Pléiade], 1959), 1:30. Unless otherwise indicated, all translations are my own.

[3] *Les Confessions*, 327.

[4] Ibid.

[5] Rousseau to Daniel Roguin, July 9, 1745, in *Correspondance complète de Jean-Jacques Rousseau*, ed. Robert Leigh (Geneva: Institut et musée Voltaire, 1965–1998), 2:84–85.

[6] "Epitre à M. de l'Etang," in *Œuvres complètes*, 2:1150.

[7] *Les Confessions*, 348.

[8] Ibid.

[9] As quoted by Robert Leigh in *Correspondance complète*, 2:163.

[10] *Discours sur les sciences et les arts*, in *Œuvres complètes*, 3:7.

[11] Ibid.

[12] *Les Confessions*, 388.

[13] Jean-Jacques Burlamaqui, *Principes du droit politique* (Geneva: Barillot et fils, 1751), xxix.

[14] "Société," in *Encyclopédie ou Dictionnaire raisonné des sciences, des arts et des métiers*, ed. Denis Diderot and Jean Le Rond d'Alembert (Paris: Briasson, 1751–1765), 15:253–54.

[15] John Locke, *Two Treatises of Government*, ed. Peter Laslett (Cambridge, U.K.: Cambridge University Press, 2002), 276.

[16] Daniel Gordon, *Citizens without Sovereignty: Equality and Sociability in French Thought, 1670–1789* (Princeton, N.J.: Princeton University Press, 1994).

[17] Samuel Pufendorf, *On the Duty of Man and Citizen*, ed. James Tully, trans. Michael Silverthorne (Cambridge, U.K.: Cambridge University Press, 2000), 35.

[18] Locke, *Two Treatises of Government*, 278.

[19] "Société," 252.

[20] On the emergence of such theories, see Ronald Meek, *Social Science and the Ignoble Savage* (New York: Cambridge University Press, 1976).

[21] See the articles "souverains," "gouvernement," and "état de nature."

[22] George-Louis Leclerc de Buffon's *Histoire naturelle, générale et particulière* (Paris: Imprimerie Royale) came out in forty-four volumes between 1749 and 1804; Antoine-François Prévost's *Histoire générale des voyages* (Paris: Didot) was published in nineteen volumes between 1746 and 1779.

[23] On this concept, see Arthur Lovejoy, *The Great Chain of Being: A Study of the History of an Idea* (Cambridge, Mass.: Harvard University Press, 1936).

[24] Rousseau further developed his ideas on language in his *Essay on the Origin of Language*.

[25] But compare Hobbes, *On the Citizen*, chap. 9. See Carole Pateman, *The Sexual Contract* (Stanford, Calif.: Stanford University Press, 1988).

[26] Pufendorf, *On the Duty of Man and Citizen*, 121.

[27] Locke, *Two Treatises of Government*, 321.

[28] Genesis 3:16.

[29] Roger Tisserand, *Les concurrents de J.-J. Rousseau à l'Académie de Dijon* (Vesoul: Imprimerie Nouvelle, 1936), essays 7 and 8.

[30] Ibid., 155.

[31] Raymond Trousson, *Jean-Jacques Rousseau jugé par ses contemporains. Du Discours sur les sciences et les arts aux Confessions* (Paris: Honoré Champion, 2000), 89, 93.

[32] François-Marie Arouet de Voltaire to Rousseau, August 30, 1755, *Correspondance complète*, 3:156–57.

[33] George Havens, *Voltaire's Marginalia on the Pages of Rousseau* (New York: Burt Franklin, 1971), 4–28.

[34] Paul Henri Thiry d'Holbach, *La morale universelle ou Les devoirs de l'homme fondés sur sa nature* (Amsterdam: M. M. Rey, 1776), 2:112. See also Holbach's *Système social* (London, 1773), 2:145.

[35] See Walter Rex, "On the Background of Rousseau's *First Discourse*," in *Studies in Eighteenth Century Culture* 9 (1979): 131–50.

[36] Du Pan to Rousseau, in *Correspondance complète*, 3:136.

[37] *Les Confessions*, 407 and 388.

[38] See Christopher Kelly, *Rousseau's Exemplary Life: The "Confessions" as Political Philosophy* (Ithaca, N.Y.: Cornell University Press, 1987), for an excellent explanation of how Rousseau's autobiography relates to his political philosophy.

[39] *Œuvres complètes*, 4:323.

Discourse on the Origin and Foundations of Inequality among Men

By Jean-Jacques Rousseau, Citizen of Geneva

Not in corrupt things, but in those which are well ordered in accordance with nature, should one consider that which is natural. Aristot[le,] Politic[s,] Bk. 2

Dedication

To the Republic of Geneva,
Magnificent, Most Honored and Sovereign Lords,

Convinced that only the virtuous citizen should present to his fatherland the honors that it can acknowledge, I have been working for thirty years to deserve to offer you a public homage, and as this happy occasion makes up in part for what my efforts have been unable to accomplish, I thought I might be permitted here to call upon the zeal that animates me more than the right that should authorize me. Having had the good fortune of being born among you, how could I meditate upon the equality that nature established among men and upon the inequality that they have instituted, without thinking of the profound wisdom with which one and the other, happily combined in this state, contribute in the manner closest to natural law and most favorable to society, to the maintenance of public order and the happiness of individuals? While seeking the best maxims on the constitution of a government that good sense could dictate, I was so struck to see them all in practice in yours that, even if I had not been born within your walls, I would have thought it impossible to refrain from offering this picture of human society to that people which, among all others, seems to me to possess the greatest advantages and to have best prevented abuses.

If I had had to choose my place of birth, I would have chosen a society limited by the extent of human faculties, that is, limited by the possibility of being well governed and in which each person being equal to his task, no one would have been constrained to commit to others the functions with which he was entrusted: a state where, since all individuals know each other, neither the obscure maneuvers of vice nor the modesty of virtue would be hidden from the eyes and judgment of the public, and where that sweet habit of seeing each other, and knowing each other, turned love of the fatherland into love of the citizens rather than that of the soil.

I would have wanted to be born in a country where the sovereign and the people could have only one and the same interest, so that all the movements of the machine always tended only to the common happiness; since that would not be possible unless the people and the sovereign were the same person, it follows that I would have wanted to be born under a democratic government, wisely tempered.

I would have wanted to live and die free, that is to say, so subject to the laws that neither I nor anyone else could shake off their honorable yoke; that salutary and gentle yoke, which the proudest heads bear with all the more docility because they are made to carry no other.

I would have wanted, therefore, that no one in the state could claim to be above the law, and that no one outside could impose any law that the state was obliged to recognize. For whatever the constitution of a government may be, if there is a single man who is not subject to the law, all the others are necessarily at his discretion (I);[1] and if there is a national leader and another foreign leader, whatever division of authority they may make, it is impossible for both of them to be well obeyed and for the state to be well governed.

I would not have wanted to live in a newly instituted republic, however good its laws might be, for fear that, if the government were perhaps constituted differently than it should have been under the circumstances, either by being unsuited to the new citizens or by the citizens being unsuited to the new government, the state would be liable to being disturbed and destroyed almost from its birth. For freedom is like those solid and rich foods, or those hearty wines, which are suited to nourish and fortify robust constitutions who are used to them, but which

---

[1] Rousseau's notes, of which this is the first, are to be found beginning on page 95.

overwhelm, ruin and intoxicate the weak and delicate who are unsuited for them. Once peoples are accustomed to masters they are no longer able to do without them. If they try to shake off the yoke, they move all the farther away from freedom because, mistaking it for an unbridled license which is its opposite, their revolutions almost always deliver them to seducers who only make their chains heavier. The Roman people itself, that model of all free peoples, was not capable of governing itself when it emerged from the oppression of the Tarquins.[2] Debased by slavery and the ignominious labors that the Tarquins had imposed on it, it was at first only a stupid mob that had to be handled and governed with the greatest wisdom, so that, growing accustomed little by little to breathe the salutary air of freedom, those souls, enervated or rather brutalized under tyranny, acquired by degrees that severity of *mœurs*[3] and that proud courage that eventually made them the most respectable of all peoples. I would therefore have sought for my fatherland a happy and quiet republic, whose antiquity was somehow lost in the darkness of time, which had experienced only such attacks as served to display and strengthen courage and love of fatherland in its inhabitants, and where the citizens, long accustomed to wise independence, were not only free, but worthy of being so.

I would have wanted to choose for myself a fatherland diverted from the ferocious love of conquests by a fortunate impotence, and safeguarded by an even more fortunate location from the fear of becoming itself the conquest of another state: a free city, situated amidst several peoples none of whom had an interest in invading it, while each had an interest in preventing the others from invading it themselves, a republic, in a word, which did not tempt the ambition of its neighbors and which could reasonably count on their help if needed. It follows that, in such a fortunate position, it would have had nothing to fear except from itself, and that, if its citizens were trained in the use of arms, it would have been to maintain among themselves that warlike ardor and that proud courage that suit freedom so well and whet the appetite for it, by the necessity to provide for their own defense.

I would have sought a country where the right of legislation was common to all citizens; for who can know better than they under which

---

[2] The Tarquins were a Roman dynasty that ended with the establishment of the Republic in ca. 509 B.C.E.

[3] The eighteenth-century French word *mœurs* has no modern-day English equivalent, which is why it is left untranslated in the text. The word refers to both manners and morals simultaneously—in other words, to beliefs and actions moderated by human customs.

conditions it suits them to live together in one society? But I would not have approved of plebiscites[4] similar to those of the Romans where the heads of state and those most interested in its conservation were excluded from the deliberations upon which its safety often depended and where, by an absurd inconsistency, the magistrates[5] were deprived of the rights enjoyed by the ordinary citizens.

On the contrary, I would have wished that, in order to stop self-interested and ill-conceived projects, and the dangerous innovations that finally ruined the Athenians, everyone did not have the power to propose new laws according to his fancy; that this right belonged to the magistrates alone, that even they used it with such circumspection that the people, on its side, was so cautious in giving its consent to these laws, and that their announcement could only take place with so much solemnity, that before the constitution could be disturbed, one had the time to realize that it is above all the great antiquity of the laws that makes them holy and venerable, and that the people soon disdains those it sees change daily, and that in growing accustomed to neglecting old ways on the pretext of doing better, great evils are often introduced in order to correct minor ones.

Above all, I would have fled, as necessarily badly governed, a republic where the people, believing it could do without its magistrates or only allowing them a precarious authority, imprudently had retained the administration of civil affairs and the execution of its own laws; such must have been the rude constitution of the first governments emerging immediately out of the state of nature and such was also one of the vices that ruined the republic of Athens.

But I would have chosen one where private persons being content to give sanction to the laws, and to decide as a body and upon the report of their leaders the most important public affairs, would establish respected tribunals, distinguish carefully their various departments; elect from year to year the most capable and most upright of their fellow citizens to administrate justice and govern the state; and where, the virtue of the magistrates thus bearing witness to the wisdom of the people, they would honor one another mutually. So that if ever some fatal misunderstandings happened to disturb public concord, even such times of blindness and error would be marked by proofs of moderation, reciprocal esteem and of a common respect for the laws, harbingers and guarantees of a sincere and perpetual reconciliation.

---

[4]A plebiscite is a direct vote in which the entire electorate accepts or rejects a proposal.
[5]Magistrates are government officials.

MAGNIFICENT, MOST HONORED AND SOVEREIGN LORDS, such are the advantages that I would have sought in the fatherland I would have chosen for myself. And if providence had in addition given it a charming site, a temperate climate, a fertile countryside, and the most delightful appearance under heaven, to complete my happiness I would have desired nothing more than to enjoy all these things in the bosom of that happy fatherland, living peacefully in sweet society with my fellow citizens, practicing toward them, and following their example, humanity, friendship and all the virtues, and leaving behind me the honorable memory of a good man and an honest and virtuous patriot.

If, less lucky or too late grown wise, I would see myself reduced to end an infirm and languishing career in other climes, uselessly regretting the quiet and peace of which an imprudent youth had deprived me, I would at least have nourished in my soul those same sentiments I could not use in my fatherland and, imbued by a tender and disinterested affection for my distant fellow citizens, from the bottom of my heart, I would have addressed to them approximately the following discourse.

My dear fellow citizens or rather my brothers, since the bonds of blood as well as the laws unite almost all of us, it gives me pleasure that I cannot think of you without at the same time thinking of all the good things you enjoy, and of which perhaps none of you feels the value better than I, who have lost them. The more I reflect upon your political and civil situation, the less I can imagine that the nature of human things could admit of a better one. In all other governments, when the question is to assure the greatest good of the state, everything is always limited to ideas of projects and at most to simple possibilities. As for you, your happiness is all established, it is only necessary to enjoy it, and to become perfectly happy you have no other need than to know how to be satisfied being so. Your sovereignty, acquired or recovered at sword's point, and preserved through two centuries by dint of valor and wisdom, is at last fully and universally recognized. Honorable treaties determine your boundaries, secure your rights and strengthen your tranquility. Your constitution is excellent, dictated by the most sublime reason and guaranteed by friendly and respectable powers. Your state is calm; you have neither wars nor conquerors to fear; you have no other masters except the wise laws you have made, administered by upright magistrates of your choosing; you are neither rich enough to enervate yourself by softness and lose in vain delights the taste for real happiness and solid virtues, nor poor enough to need more foreign help than your industry procures for you. And this precious freedom, which in large nations is maintained only by exorbitant taxes, costs you almost nothing to preserve.

For the happiness of its citizens and the example of peoples, may a republic so wisely and so happily constituted endure forever! This is the only wish left for you to make, and the only precaution left for you to take. From now on it is for you alone, not to create your happiness, since your ancestors have saved you the trouble, but to make it lasting by the wisdom of using it well. It is upon your perpetual unity, your obedience to the laws, your respect for their ministers that your preservation depends. If there remains among you the slightest germ of bitterness or distrust, hasten to destroy it as a deadly leaven which sooner or later would result in your misfortunes and the ruin of the state. I implore all of you to look deep into your hearts and consult the secret voice of your conscience. Does anyone among you know anywhere in the universe a more upright, more enlightened, more respectable body than that of your magistrates? Do not all of its members give you the example of moderation, of simplicity of *mœurs*, of respect for the laws, and of the most sincere reconciliation? Then give such wise leaders, without reserve, that salutary confidence which reason owes to virtue; bear in mind that they are of your choosing, that they justify it, and that the honors due to those whom you have established in dignity necessarily reflect back upon yourselves. None of you is so unenlightened as to be ignorant of the fact that where the vigor of the laws and the authority of their defenders cease, there can be neither security nor freedom for anyone. What, then, is at issue among you except to do wholeheartedly and with just confidence what you should always be obliged to do by a true self-interest, by duty and for the sake of reason? May a guilty and fatal indifference to the maintenance of the constitution never cause you to neglect in case of need the wise advice of the most enlightened and zealous among you. But may equity, moderation, and the most respectful firmness continue to regulate all your actions and display in you, before the whole universe, the example of a proud and modest people as jealous of its glory as of its liberty. Above all, beware, and this will be my last counsel, of ever listening to sinister interpretations and venomous discourses, whose secret motives are often more dangerous than the acts that are their object. An entire household awakens and takes warning at the first cries of a good and faithful guardian that never barks except at the approach of robbers; but people hate the importunity of those noisy animals that continually trouble public tranquility and whose continual and misplaced warnings are not heeded even at the moment when they are necessary.

And you MAGNIFICENT AND MOST HONORED LORDS; you worthy and respectable magistrates of a free people; permit me to offer my homage and respect to you in particular. If there is in the world a rank suited to confer honor on those who hold it, it is without a doubt the rank bestowed by talents and virtue, the rank of which you have proved yourselves worthy, and to which your fellow citizens have raised you. Their own merit adds further luster to yours, and I find that for having been chosen to govern them by men capable of governing others, you are as much above other magistrates, as a free people, and especially the free people you have the honor to lead, is, by its enlightenment and reason, above the populace of other states.

Allow me to cite an example of which there ought to be better records, and which will always be present in my heart. I never recall without the sweetest emotion the memory of the virtuous citizen to whom I owe my being, and who often spoke to me in my childhood of the respect that was due you. I see him still, living from the work of his hands, and nourishing his soul with the most sublime truths. I see Tacitus, Plutarch and Grotius[6] mingled before him with the instruments of his trade. I see at his side a beloved son receiving with too little profit the tender instructions of the best of fathers. But if the aberrations of a foolish youth made me forget for a while such wise lessons, I am happy to feel at last that, no matter what inclination one might have for vice, it is difficult for an education in which the heart is involved to remain lost forever.

Such are, MAGNIFICENT AND MOST HONORED LORDS, the citizens and even the simple inhabitants born in the state you govern: such are those educated and sensible men about whom, under the name of workers and people, those in other nations have such base and false ideas. My father, I gladly admit, was not distinguished among his fellow citizens; he was only what they all are and such as he was there is no country where his company would not have been sought after, cultivated, and even profitably so, by the most respectable people. It does not behoove me and, thank heaven, it is not necessary, to speak to you of the consideration men of that stamp can expect from you, your equals by education and by the rights of nature and of birth; your inferiors by their own will, by the preference they owe to your merit, which they have accorded it, and for which you, in turn, owe them a kind of gratitude. I learn with real satisfaction how much you temper toward them, by gentleness and condescension, the gravity suited to ministers of the laws; how much you reciprocate in esteem and attentions what they owe

[6]Tacitus (ca. 56–ca. 117 C.E.) was a senator and historian of the Roman Empire who wrote histories of the period; Plutarch (ca. 46–120 C.E.) was a Greek biographer; Hugo Grotius (ca. 1583–1645) was a Dutch legal scholar who wrote on natural law.

you in obedience and respect; such conduct full of justice and wisdom is apt to push further and further away the memory of the unfortunate events which must be forgotten so that they may never be seen again: Such conduct is all the more judicious as this equitable and generous people makes a pleasure of its duty, as it naturally loves to honor you, and as the most ardent in upholding their rights are the most inclined to respect yours.

It should not be surprising that the leaders of a civil society love its glory and happiness; but it is too much so for men's peace of mind that those who look upon themselves as the magistrates, or rather as the masters of a more holy and more sublime fatherland, show some love for the terrestrial fatherland that sustains them. How sweet it is for me to be able to make such a rare exception in our favor, and to rank among our best citizens those zealous trustees of the sacred dogmas authorized by the laws, those venerable pastors of souls, whose lively and sweet eloquence carries the maxims of the Gospel the better into hearts since they always begin by practicing them themselves! Everyone knows with what success the great art of the pulpit is cultivated in Geneva; however, too accustomed to seeing things spoken of in one way and done in another, few people know to what an extent the spirit of Christianity, saintliness of *mœurs*, severity toward oneself and gentleness toward others, prevail in the body of our ministers. Perhaps it falls to the city of Geneva alone to provide the edifying example of such a perfect union between a society of theologians and of men of letters. It is in great part upon their wisdom and recognized moderation, and upon their zeal for the prosperity of the state that I ground hope for its eternal tranquility; and I note with a pleasure mixed with surprise and respect, how much they abhor the frightful maxims of those sacred and barbarous men of whom history provides more than one example, and who, in order to uphold the supposed rights of God, that is to say, their own interests, were all the less sparing of human blood because they flattered themselves that their own would always be respected.

Could I forget that precious half of the republic which causes the other's happiness, and whose sweetness and wisdom maintain peace and good *mœurs* in it? Amiable and virtuous female citizens, it will always be the lot of your sex to govern ours. How fortunate when your chaste power, exercised in conjugal union alone, makes itself felt solely for the glory of the state and the public happiness: That is how the women commanded in Sparta, and that is how you deserve to command in Geneva. What could be so barbarous as to resist the voice of honor and reason from the mouth of a tender wife; and who would not despise vain luxury, upon seeing your simple and modest attire, which, by the luster it derives from you, seems the most favorable to beauty? It is up to you, always to maintain, by your amiable and innocent empire and by your subtle wit, the love of the laws in the state and concord among the citizens; to reunite divided families by happy marriages; and especially by the persuasive sweetness of your lessons and the modest graces of your conversation, to correct the extravagances our young people adopt in other countries, from which, instead of the many useful things that could profit them, they only bring back, with a childish tone and ridiculous airs picked up among lost women, an admiration for I know not what pretended grandeurs, the frivolous compensations for servitude, which will never match the value of august freedom. So be always what you are, the chaste guardians of *mœurs* and the gentle bonds of peace, and continue to assert the rights of the heart and of nature on behalf of duty and virtue.

I flatter myself that events will not prove me wrong when I base the hope for the citizens' common happiness and the republic's glory on such guarantors. I admit that, for all of these advantages, it will not glitter with the brilliance by which most eyes are dazzled, and the childish and fatal taste for which is the most mortal enemy of happiness and freedom. Let a dissolute youth go elsewhere to find easy pleasures and lasting remorse; let supposed people of taste admire elsewhere the grandeur of palaces, the beauty of carriages, the superb furnishings, the pomp of spectacles and all the refinements of softness and luxury. In Geneva will be found only men, but such a spectacle has its value, and those who will seek it will certainly be worth more than the admirers of the rest.

MAGNIFICENT, MOST HONORED AND SOVEREIGN LORDS, deign to accept, with the same goodness, the respectful testimonies of the interest I take in your common prosperity. If, in this lively outpouring of my heart, I were so unfortunate as to be guilty of some indiscreet transport, I beg you to forgive it as the tender affection of a true patriot, and as the ardent and legitimate zeal of a man who envisages no greater happiness for himself than that of seeing all of you happy.

> I am, with the deepest respect,
> MAGNIFICENT, MOST HONORED AND SOVEREIGN LORDS,
> Your most humble and most obedient servant and fellow citizen,
>
> Jean-Jacques Rousseau
> At Chambéry, June 12, 1754

Preface

The most useful and least advanced of all human knowledge seems to me to be that of man (II), and I dare say that the inscription on the Temple at Delphi[7] alone contained a more important and more difficult precept than all the great books of the moralists. Thus, I regard the subject of this discourse as one of the most interesting questions that philosophy might propose, and unfortunately for us, one of the thorniest that philosophers might resolve. For how can the source of inequality among men be known unless one begins by understanding men themselves? And how will man succeed in seeing himself as nature formed him, through all the changes that the succession of time and things must have produced in his original constitution, and to untangle what he owes to his own stock from what circumstances and his progress have added or changed in his primitive state? Like the statue of Glaucus,[8] which time, sea and storms had so disfigured that it looked less like a god than a wild beast, the human soul, altered in the midst of society by a thousand continually recurring causes, by the acquisition of a mass of knowledge and errors, by changes that have taken place in the constitution of bodies, and by the continual impact of the passions, has, so to speak, changed in appearance to the point of being almost unrecognizable; and, instead of acting always according to certain and invariable principles, instead of that celestial and majestic simplicity with which its author had endowed it, one no longer finds anything except the ugly contrast of passion which presumes to reason and understanding in a state of delirium.

What is even more cruel is that, since all the progress of the human species continually moves it farther away from its primitive state, the more new knowledge we accumulate, the more we deprive ourselves of the means of acquiring the most important knowledge of all, so that it is, in a sense, by studying man that we have made ourselves incapable of knowing him.

It is easy to see that it is in these successive changes to the human constitution that one must seek the first origin of the differences that distinguish men, who, by a common avowal, are naturally as equal among themselves as were the animals of each species, before various physical causes introduced into some species the varieties that we notice among

---

[7] The Temple of Apollo at Delphi, erected in the fourth century B.C.E., was inscribed with the saying "Know Thyself."

[8] Glaucus was a fisherman who became a sea god; he is traditionally depicted in paintings and sculptures encrusted with barnacles and covered with seaweed.

them. In fact, it is not conceivable that these first changes, however they came about, altered all the individuals of the species all at once and in the same way; rather, while some were perfected or deteriorated and acquired various good or bad qualities which were not inherent in their nature, the others remained in their original state for a longer time; and such was the first source of inequality among men, which it is easier to establish in general like this than it is to assign its true causes with precision.

Let my readers not imagine, therefore, that I dare flatter myself with having seen what appears to me so difficult to see. I have begun some arguments; I have hazarded some conjectures, less in the hope of resolving the question than with the intention of clarifying it and reducing it to its true state. Others will easily be able to go farther along the same road, although it will not be easy for anyone to reach the end. For it is no light undertaking to disentangle what is original from what is artificial in man's present nature, and to actually know a state that no longer exists, that perhaps never existed, that will probably never exist, and about which it is nevertheless necessary to have correct notions in order to judge our present state properly. Whoever might undertake to ascertain exactly the precautions required to make solid observations on this subject would need even more philosophy than is generally thought; and a good solution to the following problem would not seem to me unworthy of the Aristotles and Plinys[9] of our century. *What experiments would be necessary in order to arrive at knowledge of natural man? And by what means can such experiments be conducted in the midst of society?* Far from undertaking to resolve this problem, I believe that I have pondered the subject enough to dare answer in advance that the greatest philosophers will not be too good to direct these experiments, nor the most powerful sovereigns to conduct them; a collaboration which it is hardly reasonable to expect, especially in conjunction with the sustained or rather the successive enlightenment and good will necessary, on one side and the other, to achieve success.

This research, so difficult to conduct, and about which there has been so little thought until now, is nevertheless the only way we have left to remove a multitude of difficulties that hide from us knowledge of the real foundations of human society. It is this ignorance of the nature of man that casts so much uncertainty and obscurity on the true definition

---

[9] Aristotle (384–322 B.C.E.) was a Greek philosopher; Pliny the Elder (ca. 23–79 C.E.) was a celebrated Roman author who wrote an encyclopedic work on natural history.

of natural right: For the idea of right, says Mr. Burlamaqui,[10] and even more that of natural right, are manifestly ideas relative to the nature of man. It is therefore from this very nature of man, he continues, from his constitution and his state, that the principles of this science must be deduced.

It is not without surprise and scandal that one notices the little agreement that prevails on this important matter among the various authors who have treated it. Among the most serious writers, scarcely two can be found who are of the same opinion on this point. To say nothing of the ancient philosophers, who seem to have made a point of contradicting one another on the most fundamental principles, the Roman jurists[11] subject man and all other animals indifferently to the same natural law, because they consider under this name the law that nature imposes on itself rather than the one it prescribes, or rather, because of the particular meaning these jurists ascribed to the word *law*, which on this occasion they seem to have taken only for the expression of the general relations established by nature among all animate beings for their common preservation. The moderns, recognizing under the name *law* only a rule prescribed to a moral being, that is to say a being that is intelligent, free, and considered in its relations with other beings, consequently limit the province of natural law to the only animal endowed with reason, that is to say man; but while each one of them defines this law in his own fashion, they all base it on such metaphysical principles that, even among us, there are very few people capable of understanding these principles, let alone capable of discovering them by themselves. So that all the definitions of these wise men, which otherwise constantly contradict one another, agree only in this, that it is impossible to understand the law of nature and hence to obey it without being a great reasoner and a profound metaphysician. Which means precisely that in order to establish society men must have used an enlightenment that develops only with much difficulty and in only very few people in the midst of society itself.

Knowing nature so little and agreeing so poorly on the meaning of the word *law*, it would be very difficult to agree on a good definition of natural law. Thus all those that are found in books, besides not being uniform, have the further defect of being drawn from several kinds of knowledge which men do not naturally have, and from advantages which men can conceive of only after having left the state of nature.

---

[10] Jean-Jacques Burlamaqui (1694–1748) was a Genevan legal scholar who wrote on natural law and the social contract.
[11] Jurists are legal experts.

Writers begin by seeking the rules on which, for the common utility, it would be appropriate for men to agree among themselves; and then they give the name *natural law* to the collection of these rules, without further proof than the good that they gather would result from their universal practice. This is surely a very convenient way of composing definitions and of explaining the nature of things by almost arbitrary expediencies.

But as long as we do not know natural man, we will try in vain to determine the law that he has received or that best suits his constitution. All we can see very clearly concerning this law is that, for it to be law, not only must the will of the person whom it obligates be able to submit to it knowingly, but also, for it to be natural, it must speak directly by the voice of nature.

Leaving aside, therefore, all the scientific books that only teach us to see men as they have made themselves, and pondering the first and most simple operations of the human soul, I believe I perceive in it two principles anterior to reason, of which one interests us ardently in our well-being and our self-preservation, and the other inspires in us a natural repugnance to seeing any sentient being perish or suffer, especially our fellow human beings. It is from the conjunction and combination that our mind is able to make between these two principles, without it being necessary to introduce that of sociability, that all the rules of natural right seem to me to flow; rules that reason is subsequently forced to reestablish on other foundations, when, by its successive developments, it has succeeded in smothering nature.

This way one is not obliged to make a philosopher of man before making him a man. His duties toward others are not dictated to him solely by the belated lessons of wisdom, and as long as he does not resist the inner impulse of commiseration, he will never harm another man or even another sentient being, except in the legitimate case when, his preservation being involved, he is obliged to give himself preference. By this means, the ancient disputes about whether animals participate in natural law are also ended. For it is clear that, being devoid of enlightenment and freedom, they cannot recognize that law; but since they in some measure partake in our nature by the sentience with which they are endowed, it will be judged that they too ought to participate in natural right, and that man is subject to some sort of duties toward them. It seems, in fact, that if I am obliged not to harm my fellow man, it is less because he is a reasonable being than because he is a sentient being: a quality that, since it is common to beast and man, ought at least to give the beast the right not to be uselessly mistreated by man.

This same study of original man, of his true needs, and of the fundamental principles of his duties, is also the only effective means available to dispel the numerous difficulties surrounding the origin of moral inequality, the true foundations of the body politic, the reciprocal rights of its members, and a thousand similar questions, as important as they are badly elucidated.

When human society is viewed with a calm and disinterested eye, it seems at first to exhibit only the violence of powerful men and the oppression of the weak; the mind rebels at the hardness of the former; one is inclined to deplore the blindness of the others. And since nothing is less stable among men than those external relationships that are more often the product of chance than of wisdom, and that are called weakness or power, wealth or poverty, human establishments seem at first glance to be founded on piles of quicksand; it is only by examining them closely, it is only after removing the dust and sand that surround the edifice, that one perceives the unshakable base upon which it is raised, and that one learns to respect its foundations. Now, without the serious study of man, of his natural faculties, and of their successive developments, one will never succeed in making these distinctions and in separating what, in the present constitution of things, divine will has done, from what human art has pretended to do. The political and moral research occasioned by the important question I am examining is therefore useful in every way, and the hypothetical history of governments is in all respects an instructive lesson for man. By considering what we would have become, if we had been abandoned to ourselves, we must learn to bless him whose beneficent hand, correcting our institutions and giving them an unshakable base, prevented the disorders that must otherwise have resulted from them, and has caused our happiness to be born from the means that seemed bound to complete our misery.

> *Quem te Deus esse*
> *Jussit, et humanâ quâ parte locatus es in re*
> *Disce.*[12]

Notice about the Notes

I have added some notes to this work according to my lazy habit of working in fits and starts. These notes sometimes stray so far from the subject that they are not good to read together with the text. I therefore

---

[12] "Learn what God has ordered you to be, and what your place is in the human world." Rousseau here cites Persius (34–62 C.E.), a Roman poet and satirist who preached a stoic morality. The quotation is from *Satires* III.

cast them to the end of the discourse, in which I tried my best to follow the straightest road. Those who will have the courage to start over again can amuse themselves the second time with beating the bushes and trying to go through the notes; there will be no harm in the others' not reading them at all.

Discourse on the Origin and Foundations of Inequality among Men

It is of man that I am to speak, and the question I am examining tells me that I am going to be speaking to men; for such questions are not proposed by those who are afraid of honoring the truth. I will therefore defend with confidence the cause of humanity before the wise men who invite me to do so, and I will not be dissatisfied with myself if I prove worthy of my subject and my judges.

I conceive of two sorts of inequality in the human species: one which I call natural or physical, because it is established by nature, and which consists in the differences of age, health, strengths of body, and qualities of mind or soul; the other which one could call moral or political inequality, because it depends on a sort of convention and is established, or at least authorized, by the consent of men. The latter consists in the different privileges that some men enjoy to the prejudice of others, such as being richer, more honored, more powerful than they, or even making themselves obeyed by them.

One cannot ask what is the source of natural inequality, because the answer would be found in the simple definition of the word. Still less can one inquire if there would not be some essential link between the two inequalities; for that would be asking, in other terms, if those who command are necessarily better than those who obey, and whether the strength of the body or of the mind, wisdom or virtue, are always found in the same individuals, in proportion to power or wealth: a question perhaps good for slaves to discuss within hearing distance of their masters, but not suitable for reasonable and free men who seek the truth.

Precisely what, then, is at issue in this discourse? To mark, in the progress of things, the moment when, right replacing violence, nature was subjected to law; to explain by what marvelous chain of events the strong could resolve to serve the weak, and the people to buy an imaginary peace at the price of real felicity.

The philosophers who have examined the foundations of society have all felt it necessary to return as far back as the state of nature, but none of them has reached it. Some have not hesitated to ascribe to man in that state the notion of the just and the unjust, without bothering to show that he must have had that notion, or even that it would have been useful to him. Others have spoken of the natural right that each person has

42

to preserve what belongs to him, without explaining what they meant by belonging. Still others, first giving the stronger authority over the weaker, had government arise immediately, without thinking of the time that must have elapsed before the words *authority* and *government* could have meaning among men. Finally, all of them, speaking continually of need, avarice, oppression, desires, and pride, transported to the state of nature ideas they acquired in society: They spoke of savage man and they described civil man. It did not even enter the minds of most of our philosophers to doubt that the state of nature had existed, even though it is evident from reading the Holy Scriptures that the first man, having received some enlightenment and precepts directly from God, was not himself in that state, and that, if the writings of Moses[13] are given the credence that every Christian philosopher owes them, it must be denied that, even before the flood, men were ever in the pure state of nature, unless they fell back into it because of some extraordinary event: a paradox that is very embarrassing to defend and altogether impossible to prove.

Let us therefore begin by setting aside all the facts, for they do not affect the question. The research that can be pursued on this subject should not be taken for historical truths, but only for hypothetical and conditional reasonings better suited to clarify the nature of things than to show their real origin, like those our physicists make every day concerning the formation of the world. Religion commands us to believe that since God himself drew men out of the state of nature immediately after the creation, they are unequal because he wanted them to be, but it does not forbid us to form conjectures, drawn solely from the nature of man and the beings surrounding him, about what humankind could have become if it had remained abandoned to itself. That is what I am being asked, and what I propose to examine in this discourse. Since my subject concerns man in general, I will try to use a language that suits all nations, or rather, forgetting time and place, to think only of the men to whom I speak, I will imagine myself in the Lyceum of Athens,[14] repeating the lessons of my masters, with Plato and Xenocrates[15] for judges, and humankind for audience.

---

[13] The first five books of the Old Testament: Genesis, Exodus, Leviticus, Numbers, and Deuteronomy.

[14] The Lyceum was a place of learning in Athens where Aristotle taught philosophy.

[15] Plato (429–348 B.C.E.) was a Greek philosopher who advocated a society ruled by a "philosopher king" and a group of educated "guardians." Xenocrates (ca. 394–314 B.C.E.) was a disciple of the Greek philosopher and teacher Socrates and was famous for his virtue.

O man, whatever country you may come from, whatever your opinions may be, listen: Here is your history such as I have believed to read it, not in the books of your fellow men, which lie, but in nature which never lies. Everything that comes from it will be true. There will be nothing false except what I might have involuntarily put in of my own. The times of which I will speak are very far off. How you have changed from what you were! It is, so to speak, the life of your species that I will describe according to the qualities you received, which your education and your habits have been able to corrupt but have not been able to destroy. There is, I feel, an age at which the individual man would want to stop. You will seek the age at which you would wish your species had stopped. Discontented with your present state, for reasons that foretell even greater discontents for your unhappy posterity, perhaps you would want to be able to go back. And this sentiment must be the eulogy of your first ancestors, the criticism of your contemporaries, and the dread of those who have the misfortune of living after you.

First Part

However important it may be, in order to judge correctly the natural state of man, to consider him from his origin and examine him, so to speak, in the first embryo of the species, I will not follow his organization through its successive developments. I will not stop to research in the animal system what he might have been in the beginning, in order to have become in the end what he is; I will not examine whether, as Aristotle thinks, man's elongated nails were not at first hooked claws; whether he was not hairy like a bear; and whether he walked on all fours (III), his gaze, directed toward the earth and confined to a horizon of a few paces, did not determine both the character and the limits of his ideas. I will only be able to form some vague and almost imaginary conjectures on this subject: Comparative anatomy has as yet made too little progress, the observations of naturalists are as yet too uncertain for one to be able to establish on such foundations the basis of a solid argument. Therefore, without having recourse to the supernatural knowledge we have on this point, and without regard to the changes that must have occurred in the internal as well as external conformation of man as he applied his limbs to new uses and as he nourished himself on new foods, I will suppose him the same at all times as I see him today: walking on two feet, using his hands as we do ours, directing his gaze on all of nature, and measuring the vast expanse of heaven with his eyes.

By stripping this being, so constituted, of all the supernatural gifts he may have received, and of all the artificial faculties that he could only have acquired by prolonged progress; by considering him, in a word, as he must have come out of the hands of nature, I see an animal less strong than some, less agile than others, but, all things considered, the most advantageously organized of all. I see him satisfying his hunger under an oak, quenching his thirst at the first stream, finding his bed at the foot of the same tree that supplied his meal, and with that his needs are satisfied.

The earth, abandoned to its natural fertility (IV), and covered by immense forests never mutilated by the ax, offers at every step storehouses and shelters to animals of every species. Men, dispersed among them, observe and imitate their industry, and thereby raise themselves to the level of the beasts' instinct, with this advantage that whereas each species has only its own instinct, while man perhaps having none that belongs to him, appropriates them all, feeds himself equally well on the diverse foods (V) which the other animals share, and consequently finds his subsistence more easily than any of them can.

Accustomed since childhood to the inclemencies of the weather and the rigor of the seasons, hardened to fatigue, and forced, naked and unarmed, to defend their lives and their prey against other ferocious beasts, or to escape them by running, men develop a robust and almost unalterable temperament. Children, bringing into the world the excellent constitution of their fathers, and fortifying it with the same training that produced it, thus acquire all the vigor of which the human species is capable. Nature treats them precisely as the Law of Sparta[16] treated the children of citizens; it renders strong and robust those who are well constituted and makes all the others perish, thereby differing from our societies, where the state, by making children burdensome to fathers, kills them indiscriminately before their birth.

Since the body of the savage man is the only tool that he knows, he puts it to various uses of which ours are incapable for lack of practice; and it is our industry that deprives us of the strength and agility that necessity obliges him to acquire. If he had an ax, would his wrist break such strong branches? If he had a sling, would his hand throw a stone with such firmness? If he had a ladder, would he climb a tree so nimbly? If he had a horse, would he run so fast? Give civilized man the time to gather all his machines around him and there is no doubt that he will easily overcome savage man. But if you want to see an even more unequal fight, put them naked and disarmed, face to face, and you will soon recognize the advantage of constantly having all one's strength at one's disposal, of always being ready for any event, and of always carrying oneself, so to speak, entirely with one (VI).

Hobbes[17] claims that man is naturally intrepid and seeks only to attack and to fight. An illustrious philosopher[18] thinks, on the contrary,

---

[16]Sparta was a city-state in ancient Greece that became the dominant military power in the region. It was famous for its rigorous training of its youth.

[17]Thomas Hobbes (1588–1679) was an English philosopher. See Document 2.

[18]The reference is to the French political theorist Montesquieu (1689–1755) in his *Spirit of the Laws*, I, chap. 2.

and Cumberland[19] and Pufendorf[20] also affirm, that nothing is so timid as man in a state of nature, and that he is always trembling and ready to flee at the slightest noise that hits him, at the slightest movement that he perceives. That could be so for objects he does not know, and I do not doubt that he is frightened by all the new sights that present themselves to him, every time he can neither distinguish between the physical good and evil he can expect nor compare his forces with the dangers he must run: Such circumstances are rare in the state of nature, where everything proceeds in such a uniform manner and where the face of the earth is not subject to those brusque and continual changes caused by the passions and inconstancy of united peoples. But savage man, living dispersed among the animals, and early on finding himself in a position to measure himself against them, soon makes the comparison and, feeling that he surpasses them in skill more than they do him in strength, he learns not to fear them anymore. Pit a bear or a wolf against a savage who is robust, agile, courageous, as they all are, armed with stones and a good stick, and you will see that the danger will be reciprocal at the very least, and that after several similar experiences, wild beasts, who do not like to attack each other, will hardly attack man willingly, having found him to be just as ferocious as they are. With regard to animals that really do have more strength than he has skill, he is in the position of other weaker species, which nevertheless continue to subsist. With man having the advantage that, no less adept at running than they, and finding almost certain refuge in trees, he always has the option of accepting or leaving the encounter and the choice of flight or combat. Let us add that it does not appear that any animal naturally makes war on man except in the case of self-defense or extreme hunger, or bears him those violent antipathies that seem to announce that one species is destined by nature to serve as fodder for the other.

These are no doubt the reasons why negroes and savages worry so little about the wild beasts they might encounter in the woods. In this regard the Caribs of Venezuela, among others, live in the most profound security and without the slightest inconvenience. Although they are almost naked, says François Corréal,[21] they do not hesitate boldly to take their chances in the woods,

[19] Richard Cumberland (1631–1718) was an English bishop and legal scholar who wrote on natural law and the social contract.

[20] Samuel von Pufendorf (1632–1694) was a German legal scholar who wrote on natural law and the social contract. See Document 3.

[21] François Corréal (1648–1708) was a Spanish traveler who visited North and South America and authored *Voyages de François Corréal aux Indes Occidentales* (Paris, 1722).

armed only with bow and arrow; yet no one has ever heard that any of them has been devoured by beasts.[22]

Other, more formidable enemies, against which man does not have the same means of defense are the natural infirmities: childhood, old age and illnesses of all kinds, sad signs of our weakness, of which the first two are common to all animals and of which the last belongs principally to man living in society. On the subject of childhood, I even observe that the mother, since she carries her child with her everywhere, can nourish it with more facility than the females of many animals, which are forced to come and go incessantly with much fatigue, on the one hand to seek their food, and on the other to suckle or nourish their young. It is true that if the woman should perish, the child runs a great risk of perishing with her; but this danger is common to a hundred other species, whose young are for a long time unable to go and seek their nourishment themselves. And while childhood lasts longer among us, life does also, so that everything is still approximately equal on this point (VII), although there are, concerning the duration of the first age and the number of young (VIII), other rules which are not within my subject. Among the aged, who act and perspire little, the need for food diminishes with the capacity of providing for it; and since savage life keeps the gout and rheumatisms away from them, and since old age is, of all ills, the one that human assistance can least relieve, they eventually die without anyone noticing that they ceased to be and almost without noticing it themselves.

Regarding illnesses, I will not repeat the vain and false declamations made against medicine by most healthy people; but I will ask if there is any solid observation from which to conclude that in the countries where this art is most neglected, the average life span is shorter than in those where it is cultivated with the greatest care. And how could that be if we give ourselves more ills than medicine can furnish remedies? The extreme inequality in our way of life, the excess of idleness in some, the excess of labor in others, the ease with which our appetites and our sensuality are aroused and satisfied, the overly refined foods of the rich, which fill them with heat-making juices and devastate them with indigestion, the bad food of the poor, which they do not even have most of the time, and whose lack causes them greedily to overburden their stomachs when the occasion permits, the late nights, the excesses of every kind, the immoderate ecstasies of all the passions, the fatigues, and exhaustion of the mind, the innumerable sorrows and afflictions that are felt in every station of life and that perpetually gnaw away at

---

[22] Text in bold denotes additions from the 1782 edition of the Second Discourse.

people's souls: These are the fatal proofs that most of our ills are our own work and that we would have avoided almost all of them had we preserved the simple, uniform, and solitary way of life prescribed by nature. If it destined us to be healthy, then, I almost dare affirm, the state of reflection is a state against nature and the man who meditates is a depraved animal. When one thinks of the good constitution of savages, at least of those we have not ruined with our strong liquors, when one realizes that they know almost no other illnesses than wounds and old age, one is strongly inclined to think that the history of human illnesses could easily be written by following that of civil societies. Such at least is the opinion of Plato, who judges, from some of the remedies employed or approved by Podalirius and Machaon at the siege of Troy,[23] that various illnesses that should have been caused by those remedies, were not yet known at that time among men. **And Celsus reports that dieting, necessary today, was only invented by Hippocrates.**[24]

With so few sources of illness, man in the state of nature hardly needs remedies, still less doctors; in this regard too, the human species is in no worse condition than all the others; and it is easy to know from hunters whether in their expeditions they find many sick animals. They find many that have received extensive but very well healed wounds, that have had bones and even limbs broken and set again with no other surgeon than time, no other regimen than their ordinary life, and that are no less cured, for not having been tormented by incisions, poisoned by drugs, or weakened by fasts. In short, however useful well-administered medicine may be among us, it is still certain that if a sick savage, abandoned to himself, has nothing to hope for but from nature, in return he has nothing to fear other than his illness, which often makes his situation preferable to ours.

Let us therefore beware of confusing savage man with the men we have before our eyes. Nature treats all animals abandoned to its care with a partiality that seems to show how jealous it is of this right. The horse, the cat, the bull, even the donkey, are mostly taller, and all have a more robust constitution, more vigor, more strength and courage in the forests than in our houses. They lose half of these advantages when they are domesticated, and it could be said that all our care to treat and feed these animals well ends only in their degeneration. It is the same even for man: In becoming sociable and a slave he becomes weak, fearful,

---

[23] In Homer's *Iliad*, Podalirius and Machaon are healers in the Argive army fighting Troy.

[24] Celsus (ca. 25 B.C.E.–45 C.E.) was the Roman author of the first systematic treatise on medicine, *De Medicina*; the Greek Hippocrates (ca. 460–ca. 370 B.C.E.) is widely regarded as "the father of medicine."

servile; and his soft and effeminate way of life completes the enervation of both his strength and his courage. Let us add that between the savage and domestic conditions the difference from man to man must be even greater than that from beast to beast; for animal and man being treated equally by nature, all the commodities of which man gives himself more than the animals he tames are so many particular causes that make him degenerate more noticeably.

Nakedness, the lack of habitation, and the deprivation of all the useless things we believe so necessary, are therefore not such a great misfortune for these first men, nor, above all, are they such a great obstacle to their preservation. While they do not have hairy skin, they do not need it in warm countries, and in cold countries they soon learn to appropriate the skins of beasts they have overcome. While they have only two feet to run with, they have two arms to provide for their defense and their needs; their children may walk late and with difficulty, but the mothers carry them with ease, an advantage lacking in other species where the mother, when pursued, finds herself forced to abandon her young, or to adjust her pace to theirs. **There may be a few exceptions to this. For example, that animal of the province of Nicaragua that resembles a fox, has feet like the hands of a man, and, according to Corréal, has a pouch under his stomach where the mother puts her young when she is obliged to flee. This is doubtless the same animal that is called Tlaquatzin in Mexico, and to the female of which Laët[25] ascribes a similar pouch for the same use.** Finally, unless one assumes the singular and fortuitous combination of circumstances of which I will speak in the sequel and which could very well never have occurred, it is for all intents and purposes clear that he who first made himself clothes or a dwelling, thereby gave himself things that are not very necessary, since he had done without them until then, and since it is not evident why he could not have tolerated as a grown man a mode of life he had tolerated since childhood.

Alone, idle, and always near danger, savage man must like to sleep and be a light sleeper like the animals, which, since they think little, sleep, so to speak, all the time they are not thinking. His self-preservation being almost his only care, his best-trained faculties must be those whose principal object is attack and defense, either to subjugate his prey or to save himself from being the prey of another animal. By contrast, the organs that are perfected only by softness and sensuality must remain

---

[25] Jean Laët (1593–1649) was a Flemish traveler who published a book on the Americas in 1633.

in a state of coarseness which excludes any kind of delicacy in him; and since his senses differ in this regard, he will have extremely crude touch and taste; sight, hearing, and smell of the greatest subtlety. Such is the animal state in general and it is also, according to travelers' reports, that of most savage peoples. Therefore one should not be surprised that the Hottentots of the Cape of Good Hope[26] sight vessels on the high sea with their naked eyes as far away as do the Dutch with spyglasses; nor that American savages could smell Spaniards on the trail as the best dogs could have done; nor that all those barbarous nations endure their nakedness without discomfort, sharpen their taste by means of peppers, and drink European liquors like water.

Until now I have considered only physical man. Let us try to look at him from the metaphysical and moral side.

I see in any animal nothing but an ingenious machine, to which nature has given senses to wind itself up and, to guard itself, to a certain point, from all that tends to destroy or disturb it. I perceive precisely the same things in the human machine, with this difference that nature alone does everything in the operations of the beast, while man contributes to his operations in his capacity as a free agent. The one chooses or rejects by instinct, and the other by an act of liberty; so that a beast cannot deviate from the rule that is prescribed to it even when it would be advantageous for it to do so, and a man deviates from it often to his detriment. Thus a pigeon would die of hunger near a basin filled with the best meats, and a cat upon heaps of fruits or grain, although both could nourish themselves very well on the food they disdain, if they would make up their mind to try some. Thus dissolute men abandon themselves to excesses which cause them fever and death, because the mind depraves the senses and because the will still speaks when nature is silent.

Every animal has ideas, since it has senses; it even combines its ideas up to a certain point, and in this man differs from a beast only in degree. Some philosophers have even suggested that there is more difference between a given man and another than between a given man and a given animal; therefore it is not so much understanding that constitutes the specific distinction of man among the animals as it is his being a free agent. Nature commands every animal, and the beast obeys. Man experiences the same impression, but he realizes that he is free to acquiesce or to resist, and it is above all in the consciousness of this freedom that the spirituality of his soul is shown. For physics explains in some

---

[26] This is a reference to an African tribe living on the Atlantic coast of South Africa.

way the mechanism of the senses and the formation of ideas; but in the power of willing or rather of choosing, and in the sentiment of this power are found only purely spiritual acts about which the laws of mechanics explain nothing.

But if the difficulties that surround all these questions might leave some room for disagreement about this difference between man and animal, there is another very specific quality that distinguishes them and about which there can be no debate, namely the faculty of perfecting oneself; a faculty which, with the aid of circumstances, successively develops all the others and resides in us as much in the species as in the individual. By contrast an animal is, at the end of a few months, what it will be all his life, and its species is, at the end of a thousand years, what it was the first year of that thousand. Why is man alone liable to become an imbecile? Is it not that he thereby returns to his primitive state, and that, while the beast, which has acquired nothing and which has, moreover, nothing to lose, always retains its instinct, man losing again by old age or other accidents all that his *perfectibility* had made him acquire, thus falls back lower than even the beast? It would be sad for us to be forced to agree that this distinctive and almost unlimited faculty is the source of all man's misfortunes; that it is this faculty that draws him, by dint of time, out of that original condition in which he would spend calm and innocent days; that it is this faculty which, over the centuries, causes his enlightenment and his errors, his vices and his virtues, and in the long run makes him the tyrant of himself and of nature (IX). It would be horrible to be obliged to praise as a beneficent being the one who first suggested to the inhabitant of the banks of the Orinoco[27] the use of those slats which he binds on the temples of his children, and which assure them at least a part of their imbecility and original happiness.

Savage man, by nature left to instinct alone, or rather, compensated for the instinct he perhaps lacks by faculties capable of substituting for it at first, and then of raising him far above nature, will therefore begin with purely animal functions (X): to perceive and to feel will be his first state, which he will have in common with all animals. To will and not to will, to desire and to fear, will be the first and perhaps the only operations of his soul, until new circumstances cause new developments in it.

Whatever the moralists say about it, human understanding owes a lot to the passions, which, by a common agreement, also owe much to it. It is by their activity that our reason perfects itself; we seek to know only

---

[27] The Orinoco is one of the longest rivers in South America.

because we wish to enjoy, and it is not possible to conceive why a person who had neither desires nor fears would take the trouble of reasoning. The passions, in turn, derive their origin from our needs and their progress from our knowledge; for one can desire or fear things only through the ideas one can have of them, or by the simple impulse of nature; and savage man, deprived of every kind of enlightenment, experiences only passions of this last kind; his desires do not exceed his physical needs (XI); the only goods he knows in the universe are food, a female, and rest. The only evil he fears are pain and hunger. I say pain and not death because an animal will never know what it is to die; and knowledge of death and its terrors is one of the first acquisitions that man has made in moving away from the animal condition.

It would be easy for me, were it necessary, to support this sentiment by facts and to show that in all nations of the world the progress of the mind has been precisely proportioned to the needs that people received from nature or to those to which circumstances subjected them, and consequently to the passions which inclined them to provide for those needs. I would show the arts being born in Egypt and spreading with the flooding of the Nile. I would follow their progress among the Greeks, where they were seen to spring up, grow, and rise to the heavens amid the sands and rocks of Attica without being able to take root on the fertile banks of the Eurotas.[28] I would note that, in general, the people of the north are more industrious than those of the south, because they can less afford not to be, as if nature wanted to equalize things, by giving to minds the fertility it denies the soil.

But without invoking the uncertain testimonies of history, who fails to see that everything seems to remove from savage man the temptation and the means of ceasing to be savage? His imagination depicts nothing to him; his heart asks nothing of him. His modest needs are easily satisfied, and he is so far from the degree of knowledge necessary to desire greater ones that he can have neither foresight nor curiosity. The spectacle of nature becomes indifferent to him by dint of becoming familiar. There is always the same order, there are always the same revolutions; he does not have the mind to wonder at the greatest marvels; and it is not in him that the philosophy that man needs should be sought, in order to know how to observe once what he has seen every day. His soul, which nothing stirs, is given over to the sole sentiment of its present existence without any idea of the future, however near it may be, and his projects, as limited as his views, barely extend to the end of

---

[28] The Eurotas is a river in Greece.

the day. Such is, even today, the degree of foresight of the Carib: In the morning he sells his bed of cotton, and in the evening he comes weeping to buy it back, for want of having foreseen that he would need it for the next night.

The more one meditates on this subject, the more the distance from pure sensations to the most simple knowledge grows in our eyes; and it is impossible to conceive how a man could, by his strength alone, without the aid of communication, and without the stimulus of necessity, have bridged so great a divide. How many centuries perhaps elapsed before men were in a position to see another fire than that of heaven? How many different chance occurrences must they have needed before they learned the most common uses of that element? How many times did they let it die out before they acquired the art of reproducing it? And how many times did each one of these secrets perhaps die with the one who had discovered it? What shall we say about agriculture, an art that demands so much labor and foresight, which depends on so many other arts, which very obviously is practicable only in a society which has at least begun, and which serves us not so much to extract from the soil foods it would readily yield without agriculture, as to force it to satisfy preferences that are more to our taste? But let us suppose that men had multiplied so greatly that the natural produce no longer sufficed to nourish them, a supposition which, it could be said in passing, would point to one great advantage for the human species in this way of life. Let us suppose that without forges and workshops, the tools for farming had fallen from heaven into the hands of the savages, that these men had conquered the mortal hatred they all have for continuous labor, that they had learned to foresee their needs so long in advance, that they had guessed how land must be cultivated, grains sown, and trees planted, that they had discovered the art of grinding wheat and fermenting grapes—all things they would have had to be taught by the gods, as it is impossible to conceive how they could have learned them by themselves. After that, what man would be insane enough to torment himself cultivating a field that will be plundered by the first comer, whether man or beast, for whom the crop is suitable; and how can each person resolve to spend his life in hard work, when the more he needs its reward, the more certain he is of not reaping it? In a word, how can this situation possibly cause men to cultivate the earth as long as it has not been divided among them, that is to say as long as the state of nature is not annihilated?

Were we to want to suppose a savage man as skillful in the art of thinking as our philosophers make him out to be, were we, following their example, to make of him a philosopher, discovering by himself the most sublime truths, making for himself, by chains of very abstract reasoning, maxims of justice, and reason drawn from the love of order in general or from the known will of his Creator; in a word, were we to suppose his mind to be as intelligent and enlightened as it must—and, in fact, is found—to be thick and stupid, what use would the species derive from all this metaphysics, which could not be communicated and would perish with the individual who had invented it? What progress could humankind make, scattered in the woods among the animals? And how much could men mutually perfect and enlighten one another, who, having neither fixed dwelling nor any need of one another, might meet perhaps hardly twice in their life, without knowing or speaking with one other?

Let us consider how many ideas we owe to the use of speech; how much grammar trains and facilitates the operations of the mind. And let us think of the inconceivable difficulties and time the first invention of languages must have cost. If one adds these reflections to the preceding ones, then one can judge how many thousands of centuries would have been required to develop successively in the human mind the operations of which it was capable.

Permit me to consider for an instant the difficulties regarding the origin of languages. I could leave it at just quoting or restating here the research that Mr. the Abbé de Condillac[29] has conducted on this matter, which all fully confirms my sentiment and which, perhaps, gave me the first idea of it. But since the way this philosopher resolves the difficulties that he himself raises concerning the origin of instituted signs shows that he assumed what I question—namely a kind of society already established among the inventors of language—I believe, in referring to his reflections, that I ought to add to them my own, in order to present the same difficulties in the way that suits my subject. The first that presents itself is to imagine how language could have become necessary; for since men had no communication among themselves nor any need for it, one cannot conceive the necessity or the possibility of this invention were it not indispensable. I might well say, as many others do, that languages were born in the domestic exchanges of fathers, mothers, and children. But aside from the fact that this would not resolve the objections, it would be to commit the error of those who, in reasoning

---

[29]Étienne Bonnot de Condillac (1714–1780) was a French *philosophe* who published the *Essay on the Origin of Knowledge* in 1746. Here Rousseau engages some of his period's most advanced thinking on the origin of languages. He would further develop his ideas in his *Essay on the Origin of Language* (published posthumously in 1781).

about the state of nature, carry over to it ideas taken from society, and always see the family gathered in one same dwelling and its members maintaining among themselves a union as intimate and permanent as among us, where so many common interests unite them; when instead, in this primitive state, having neither house, nor huts, nor property of any kind, everyone took up his lodging by chance and often for only one night. The males and females united fortuitously depending on encounter, occasion, and desire, without speech being a very necessary interpreter of the things they had to say to each other; they left each other with the same ease (XII). The mother nursed her children at first for her own need; then, habit having endeared them to her, she nourished them afterward for theirs. As soon as they had the strength to seek their food, they did not delay in leaving even the mother; and as there was almost no other way of finding one another again than not to lose sight of each other in the first place, they were soon at the point of not even recognizing one another. Note also that since the child has all its needs to explain and hence has more things to say to the mother than the mother has to the child, it is the child that must make the greatest efforts of invention, and that the language it uses must be in great part its own work, which multiplies languages as many times as there are individuals to speak them. A wandering and vagabond life contributes further to this, since it does not give any idiom the time to gain consistency. For to say that the mother dictates to the child the words he ought to use to ask her for this or that shows well how one teaches already formed languages, but it does not teach us how they are formed.

Let us suppose this first difficulty vanquished: Let us cross over for a moment the immense space that there must have been between the pure state of nature and the need for languages. And, let us seek, assuming them to be necessary (XIII), how they might have begun to be established. New difficulty, worse still than the preceding one; for if men needed speech in order to learn to think, they had an even greater need of knowing how to think in order to discover the art of speech. And even if we understood how the sounds of the voice came to be taken for the conventional interpreters of our ideas, it would still leave open the question of what could have been the interpreters of that convention for ideas which, having no sensible object, could not be pointed to by gesture nor by voice, so that it is hardly possible to form tenable conjectures about the origin of this art of communicating thoughts and establishing commerce between minds: a sublime art which is already so far from its origin, but which the philosopher still sees at so prodigious a distance from its perfection that there is not a man bold enough to guarantee it will ever be reached, even should the revolutions time necessarily brings be suspended in its favor, even should prejudices quit the academies or fall silent before them, and should they be able to attend to this thorny topic for whole centuries without interruption.

Man's first language, the most universal, most energetic, and only language he needed before it was necessary to persuade assembled men, is the cry of nature. Since this cry was elicited only by a kind of instinct in pressing circumstances, to beg for help in great dangers, or for relief of violent ills, it was not of much use in the ordinary course of life, where more moderate sentiments prevail. When the ideas of men began to spread and multiply, and when closer communication was established among them, they sought more numerous signs and a more extensive language; they multiplied the inflections of the voice, and joined to it gestures that are more expressive by their nature, and whose meaning is less dependent on prior determination. They therefore expressed visible and mobile objects by gestures, and audible ones by imitative sounds. But because gesture indicates hardly anything except present or easily described objects and visible actions; because its usage is not universal, since darkness or the interposition of a body render it useless; and since it requires attention rather than stimulates it, men finally thought to substitute for it the articulations of the voice which, without having the same relation to certain ideas, are better suited to represent all ideas as instituted signs: a substitution which could not have been made except by common consent, and in a way rather difficult to practice for men whose crude organs as yet had no training, and even more difficult to conceive in itself, since that unanimous agreement must have had a motive, and since speech seems to have been highly necessary in order to establish the use of speech.

One must conclude that the first words men used had in their mind a much broader meaning than do those used in already formed languages; and being ignorant of the division of discourse into its constituent parts, they at first gave each word the meaning of a whole sentence. When they began to distinguish subject from attribute and verb from noun, which was no small effort of genius, substantives were at first only so many proper nouns; the **present** infinitive was the sole tense of verbs; and the notion of adjectives must have developed only with great difficulty, because every adjective is an abstract word and abstractions are difficult and not very natural operations.

Every object received at first a particular name, without regard to genus and species, which these first institutors were not in a position to distinguish; and all individual things presented themselves to their minds in isolation as they are in the spectacle of nature. If one oak tree was called A, another oak tree was called B, **for the first idea one draws from two things is that they are not the same; and often much time is needed to observe what they have in common.** So that the more limited the knowledge, the more extensive the dictionary. The obstacle of all this nomenclature could not easily be removed, for in order to organize beings under common and generic denominations, it was necessary to know their properties and differences. Observations and definitions were necessary—that is to say, much more natural history and metaphysics than the men of those times could have had.

Besides, general ideas can come into the mind only with the aid of words, and the understanding grasps them only through propositions. That is one of the reasons why animals can neither form such ideas nor ever acquire the perfectibility that depends on them. When a monkey goes without hesitating from one nut to another, is it thought that he has a general idea of this kind of fruit and that he compares its archetype to these two individuals? Undoubtedly not; but the sight of one of these nuts recalls to his memory the sensations he received from the other, and his eyes, modified in a certain way, announce to his taste the modification it is going to receive. Every general idea is purely intellectual; if imagination is in the least involved, the idea immediately becomes particular. Try to draw for yourself the image of a tree in general, you will never succeed in doing it; despite yourself it must be seen small or large, sparse or leafy, light or dark; and if it were up to you to see in it only what is found in every tree, this image would no longer resemble a tree. Purely abstract beings are seen in the same way, or are conceived only through discourse. The definition of the triangle alone gives you the true idea of it: as soon as you imagine one in your mind, it is a given triangle and not another, and you cannot avoid making its lines perceptible or its plane colored. It is therefore necessary to utter propositions, hence to speak, in order to have general ideas; for as soon as the imagination stops, the mind goes no further without the help of discourse. If, then, the first inventors could give names only to ideas they already had, it follows that the first substantives could never have been anything but proper nouns.

But when, by means that I cannot conceive, our new grammarians began to extend their ideas and to generalize their words, the ignorance of the inventors must have subjected this method to very narrow limitations; and just as at first they had overly multiplied the names of individual things for want of knowing the genera and species, they then made too few species and genera for want of having considered beings by all their differences. To extend the divisions far enough would have required more experience and enlightenment than they could have had, and more research and labor than they wanted to put into it. Now if even today new species are daily discovered that have eluded all our observations until now, think how many species must have been hidden from men who judged things only on first appearance! As for primary classes and the most general notions, it is superfluous to add that they still must have escaped them. How, for example, would they have imagined or understood the words *matter, mind, substance, mode, figure, movement*, since our philosophers, who have used them for such a long time, have much trouble understanding them themselves; and since, the ideas attached to these words being purely metaphysical, they found no model of them in nature?

I stop with these first steps, and beg my judges to suspend their reading here to consider, concerning the invention of physical substantives alone—that is to say, concerning the easiest part of the language to discover—how far language still has to go to express all the thoughts of men, assume a consistent form, be capable of being spoken in public, and influence society. I beg them to reflect upon how much time and knowledge were necessary to discover numbers (XIV), abstract words, aorists,[30] and all the tenses of verbs, particles, syntax, the linking of propositions, reasoning, and the forming of all the logic of discourse. As for myself, frightened by the multiplying difficulties, and convinced of the almost demonstrated impossibility that languages could have arisen and been established by purely human means, I leave to whomever would undertake it the discussion of the following difficult problem: Which was most necessary, previously formed society for the institution of languages, or previously invented languages for the establishment of society?

Whatever these origins may be, from the little care taken by nature to bring men together through mutual needs and to facilitate their use of speech, one at least sees how little it prepared their sociability, and how little it contributed to everything men have done to establish bonds. In fact, it is impossible to imagine why, in that primitive state, a man would sooner have need of another man than a monkey or a wolf would need its kind; or, supposing this need, what motive could induce the other to provide for it, or even, in this last case, how they might agree on terms. I know we are repeatedly told that nothing would have been as miserable as man in that state; and if it is true, as I believe I have proven, that only

---

[30]Aorists are forms of verbs in some languages.

after many centuries could man have had the desire and opportunity to leave it, then that would be an indictment of nature, and not of him who nature had so constituted. But if I understand this term *miserable* properly, it is a word that has no meaning or only signifies a painful privation and the suffering of the body or soul. Now I would really like someone to explain to me what type of misery there can be for a free being whose heart is at peace and whose body is healthy? I ask which, civil or natural life, is more liable to become unbearable to those who enjoy it? We see around us almost only people who complain about their existence, even many who deprive themselves of it insofar as they are able; and the combination of divine and human laws hardly suffices to stop this disorder. I ask if anyone has ever heard it said that a savage in freedom even dreamed of complaining about life and killing himself. Let us then judge with less pride on which side true misery lies. Nothing, on the contrary, would have been as miserable as savage man dazzled by enlightenment, tormented by passions, and reasoning about a state different from his own. For it was by a very wise providence that his potential faculties were to develop only with the opportunities to exercise them, so that they were neither superfluous and burdensome to him beforehand, nor tardy and useless when needed. He had, in instinct alone, everything necessary for him to live in the state of nature: He has, in a cultivated reason, only what is necessary for him to live in society.

It seems at first that men in that state, not having among themselves any kind of moral relationship or known duties, could be neither good nor bad and had neither vices nor virtues: unless, taking these words in a physical sense, one calls vices in the individual the qualities that can harm his own preservation, and virtues those that can contribute to it; in which case, it would be necessary to call the most virtuous the one who least resists the simple impulses of nature. But without departing from the ordinary meaning, it is appropriate to suspend the judgment we might pass on such a situation and beware of our prejudices, until it has been examined, with scale in hand, whether there are more virtues than vices among civilized men; or whether their virtues are more advantageous than their vices are deadly; or whether the progress of their knowledge is a sufficient compensation for the harms they do one another as they learn of the good they ought to do; or whether all things considered, they would not be in a happier situation having neither harm to fear nor good to hope for from anyone, rather than subjecting themselves to a universal dependence and obliging themselves to receive everything from those who do not obligate themselves to give them anything.

Above all, let us not conclude with Hobbes that because man has no idea of goodness, he is naturally evil; that he is vicious because he does not know virtue; that he always refuses his fellow men services he does not believe he owes them; nor that, by virtue of the right he reasonably claims to things he needs, he foolishly imagines himself to be the sole proprietor of the whole universe. Hobbes saw very clearly the defect of all modern definitions of natural right;[31] but the consequences he draws from his own definition show that he takes it in a sense which is no less false. Reasoning upon the principles he establishes, this author should have said that since the state of nature is that in which care for our own preservation is the least prejudicial to the self-preservation of others, it follows that this state was the most conducive to peace and the best suited to humankind. He says precisely the contrary, because of having improperly injected into the savage man's care for his preservation the need to satisfy a multitude of passions that are the product of society and which have made laws necessary. The evil man, he says, is a robust child. It remains to be seen whether savage man is a robust child. Should we grant this to him, what would he conclude from it? That if, when he is robust, this man were as dependent on others as when he is weak, there is no kind of excess to which he would not be inclined: that he would beat his mother when she would be too slow in giving him her breast; that he would strangle one of his young brothers when he would be inconvenienced by him; that he would bite another's leg when he was hit or annoyed by it. But being robust and being dependent are two contradictory suppositions in the state of nature. Man is weak when he is dependent, and he is emancipated before he is robust. Hobbes did not see that the same cause that prevents savages from using their reason, as our jurists claim, prevents them at the same time from abusing their faculties, as he himself claims. Thus one could say that savages are not evil precisely because they do not know what it is to be good; for it is neither the growth of enlightenment nor the restraint of the law, but the calm of the passions and the ignorance of vice which prevent them from doing evil: *Tanto plus in illis proficit vitiorum ignoratio, quam in his cognitio virtutis.*[32] There is, besides, another principle that Hobbes did not notice, and which—having been given to man in order to soften, under certain circumstances, the ferocity of his *amour*

---

[31] Namely, that they defined it in terms of man's being rational and sociable.

[32] "Among them the ignorance of vice is more profitable than the knowledge of virtue is among others." Rousseau here cites Justin, a third-century Roman historian who lived under the empire.

propre[33] or the desire for self-preservation before the birth of *amour propre* (XV) —tempers the ardor he has for his own well-being by an innate repugnance to see his fellow man suffer. I do not believe I have any contradiction to fear in granting man the only natural virtue that the most excessive detractor of human virtues[34] was forced to recognize. I speak of pity, a disposition that is appropriate to beings as weak and subject to as many ills as we are; a virtue all the more universal and useful to man because it precedes in him the use of all reflection; and so natural that even beasts sometimes give perceptible signs of it. Without speaking of the tenderness of mothers for their young and of the perils they brave to guard them, one observes daily the repugnance of horses to trample a living body underfoot. An animal does not pass near a dead animal of its species without uneasiness. There are even some animals that give them a kind of burial; and the sad lowing of cattle entering a slaughterhouse announces the impression they receive from the horrible sight that strikes them. One sees with pleasure the author of the *Fable of the Bees*, forced to recognize man as a compassionate and sensitive being,[35] departing from his cold and subtle style in the example he gives in order to offer us the pathetic image of an imprisoned man who sees outside a wild beast tearing a child from his mother's breast, breaking his weak limbs in its murderous teeth, and ripping apart with its claws the palpitating entrails of this child. What horrible agitation must be felt by this witness of an event in which he takes no personal interest! What anguish must he suffer at this sight, being unable to bring help to the fainting mother or to the dying child?

Such is the pure movement of nature prior to all reflection. Such is the force of natural pity, which the most depraved *mœurs* still have difficulty destroying, since daily in our theaters one sees, moved and crying for the troubles of an unfortunate person, a man who, if he were in the tyrant's place, would aggravate his enemy's torments even more, **like the bloodthirsty Sulla,**[36] **so sensitive to ills he had not caused, or like Alexander of Pherae,**[37] **who did not dare attend the perfor-**

[33] *Amour propre* means self-love. For another kind of self-love (*amour de soi-même*), see Rousseau's note XV (p. 122). The French has been kept to maintain the distinction.

[34] Rousseau is here referring to the Dutch thinker Bernard de Mandeville (1670–1733), whose scandalous *The Fable of the Bees* (1714) suggested that "private vices" could lead to "public benefits."

[35] Mandeville wrote about "pity or compassion, which consists in a fellow-feeling and condolence for the misfortunes and calamities of others: all mankind are more or less affected with it; but the weakest minds generally the most."

[36] Sulla (138–78 B.C.E.) was a Roman general, politician, and dictator.

[37] Alexander of Pherae (r. 369–358 B.C.E.) was a tyrannical ruler of ancient Greece.

mance of any tragedy for fear of being seen moaning with Andromache and Priam,[38] whereas he listened without emotion to the
cries of so many citizens murdered daily on his orders.

Mollissima corda
Humano generi dare se natura fatetur,
Quae lacrimas dedit.[39]

   Mandeville sensed very well that even with all their morality men
would never have been anything but monsters if nature had not given
them pity in support of reason; but he did not see that from this quality alone flow all the social virtues he wants to question in men. In fact,
what are generosity, clemency, humanity, if not pity applied to the weak,
to the guilty, or to the human species in general? Benevolence and even
friendship are, rightly understood, the products of a constant pity fixed
on a particular object, for is desiring that someone not suffer anything
but desiring that he be happy? Even should it be true that commiseration is only a sentiment that puts us in the position of him who suffers,
an obscure and strong sentiment in savage man, developed but weak in
civil man, what would this idea matter to the truth of what I say, except
to give it more force? In fact, commiseration will be all the more energetic as the observing animal identifies himself more intimately with
the suffering animal. Now it is evident that this identification must have
been infinitely closer in the state of nature than in the state of reasoning.
Reason engenders *amour propre*, and it is reflection that fortifies it; it is
reason that turns man back upon himself, it separates him from all that
bothers and afflicts him. It is philosophy that isolates him; it is because
of it that he says in secret, at the sight of a suffering man: Perish if you
will, I am safe. Only dangers to the entire society trouble the tranquil
sleep of the philosopher and tear him from his bed. His fellow man can
be murdered with impunity right under his window; he has only to put
his hands over his ears and argue with himself a bit to prevent nature,
which revolts within himself, from identifying him with the man who
is being assassinated. Savage man does not have this admirable talent,
and for want of wisdom and reason he is always seen heedlessly yield-
ing to the first sentiment of humanity. In riots or street fights the populace assembles, the prudent man moves away; it is the rabble, the

---

[38] Andromache and Priam are Greek mythological figures.
[39] "In giving men tears, nature bears witness that she gave the human race the softest
hearts." Rousseau is here citing the Roman poet Juvenal, who was active in the second
century C.E. and wrote a collection of satirical poems. This is from *Satire XV*.

marketwomen, who separate the combatants and prevent the cultivated people from murdering each other.

It is therefore certain that pity is a natural sentiment, which, moderating in each individual the activity of self-love, contributes to the mutual preservation of the entire species. It is pity which carries us without reflection to the aid of those whom we see suffer; it is pity which, in the state of nature, takes the place of laws, *mœurs*, and virtue, with the advantage that no one is tempted to disobey its gentle voice; it is pity which will dissuade every robust savage from robbing a weak child or an infirm old man of his hard-won subsistence, if he himself hopes to be able to find his own elsewhere. It is pity which instead of that sublime maxim of reasoned justice, *Do unto others as you would have them do unto you*, inspires all men with this other maxim of natural goodness, much less perfect but perhaps more useful than the preceding one: *Do what is good for you with the least possible harm to others*. It is, in a word, in this natural sentiment, rather than in subtle arguments, that one must seek the cause of the repugnance every man would feel in doing evil, even independently of the maxims of education. Although it may behoove Socrates and minds of his stamp to acquire virtue through reason, humankind would have perished long ago if its preservation had depended only on the reasonings of its members.

With such inactive passions and such a salutary restraint, men, more wild than evil, and more attentive to protecting themselves from harm they could receive than tempted to harm others, were not subject to very dangerous quarrels. Since they had no kind of commerce among themselves; since they consequently knew neither vanity, nor consideration, nor esteem, nor contempt; since they did not have the slightest notion of thine and mine, nor any true idea of justice; since they regarded the violence they might suffer as harm easy to redress and not as an insult which must be punished, and since they did not even dream of vengeance, except perhaps mechanically and on the spot, like the dog that bites the stone thrown at him, their disputes would rarely have had bloody consequences had there been no more sensitive subject than food. But I see a more dangerous subject left for me to discuss.

Among the passions that agitate the heart of man, there is an ardent, impetuous one that makes one sex necessary to the other; a terrible passion which braves all dangers, overcomes all obstacles, and which, in its fury, seems fit to destroy humankind when it is destined to preserve it. What must become of men, tormented by this unbridled and brutal rage, without modesty, without restraint, and daily fighting each other over their loves at the price of their blood?

It must first be agreed that the more violent the passions, the more necessary laws are to contain them. But besides the fact that the disorders and crimes these passions cause every day among us show well enough the inadequacy of laws in this regard, it would still be good to examine whether these disorders did not arise with the laws themselves; for then, even should they be capable of repressing these disorders, the very least that ought to be required of the laws is to stop an evil which would not exist without them.

Let us begin by distinguishing between the moral and the physical in the sentiment of love. The physical is that general desire which inclines one sex to unite with the other. The moral is what determines this desire and fixes it exclusively on a single object, or which at least gives it a greater degree of energy for this preferred object. Now it is easy to see that the moral element of love is an artificial sentiment born of social practice, and extolled with much skill and care by women in order to establish their ascendancy and make dominant the sex that ought to obey.[40] This sentiment, since it is based on certain notions of merit or beauty that a savage is not in a position to have, and on comparisons he is not in a position to make, must be almost nonexistent for him. For as his mind could not form abstract ideas of regularity and proportion, so his heart is not susceptible to the sentiments of admiration and love that, even without our noticing it, arise from the application of these ideas. He heeds only the temperament he received from nature, and not the taste he has not been able to acquire; any woman is good for him.

Limited solely to that which is physical in love, and fortunate enough to be ignorant of those preferences that irritate its sentiment and augment its difficulties, men must feel the ardors of their temperament less frequently and less vividly, and consequently have fewer and less cruel disputes among themselves. Imagination, which causes so much havoc among us, does not speak to savage hearts. Everyone peaceably waits for the impulsion of nature, yields to it without choice with more pleasure than frenzy; and the need satisfied, all desire is extinguished.

It is therefore incontestable that love itself, like all the other passions, has acquired only in society that impetuous ardor which so often makes it fatal for men; and it is all the more ridiculous to portray savages continually murdering each other to satisfy their brutality as this opinion is directly contrary to experience, and as the Caribs, which of all existing peoples have so far departed least from the state of nature, are precisely the most peaceful in their loves and the least subject to jealousy, even

---

[40] According to Genesis 3:16.

though they live in a burning hot climate, which always seems to give greater activity to these passions.

Regarding inferences that might be drawn, in some species of animals, from the fights of males that bloody our farmyards in all seasons or which make our forests resound with their cries in spring as they feud over a female, it is necessary to begin by excluding all species in which nature has manifestly established, in the relative power of the sexes, other relations than among us: Thus cockfights do not provide a basis for inferences about the human species. In species where proportion is better observed, the causes for these fights can only be the scarcity of females in comparison to the number of males, or the exclusive intervals during which the female consistently refuses to let the male approach her, which is equivalent to the first cause; for if each female tolerates the male during only two months of the year, in this respect it is the same as if the number of females were reduced by five-sixths. Now neither of these two cases is applicable to the human species, in which the number of females generally surpasses the number of males, and in which it has never been observed that, even among savages, females, like those of other species, have times of heat and exclusion. Moreover, among some of these animals, since the entire species enters into effervescence at the same time, there comes a terrible moment of general ardor, tumult, disorder, and fighting: a moment that does not take place in the human species, in which love is never periodic. Therefore one cannot conclude from the fights of certain animals for the possession of females that the same thing would happen to man in the state of nature. And even if one could draw that conclusion, as these dissensions do not destroy the other species, one must consider at least that they would not be more fatal to ours; and it is very apparent that they would cause still less havoc than they do in society, particularly in countries where, *mœurs* still counting for something, the jealousy of lovers and the vengeance of husbands are a daily cause of duels, murders, and worse things; where the obligation to eternal fidelity serves only to create adulterers; and where even the laws of continence and honor necessarily spread debauchery and multiply abortions.

Let us conclude that wandering in the forests, without industry, without speech, without domicile, without war and without liaisons, with no need of his fellow men, likewise with no desire to harm them, perhaps never even recognizing anyone individually, savage man, subject to few passions and self-sufficient, had only the sentiments and intellect suited to that state; he felt only his true needs, saw only what he believed he had an interest to see; and his intelligence made no more progress than his vanity. If by chance he made some discovery, he was all the less able to communicate it because he did not even recognize his children. Art perished with the inventor. There was neither education nor progress; the generations multiplied uselessly; and everyone starting always from the same point, centuries passed in all the crudeness of the first ages; the species was already old, and man remained ever a child.

If I have dwelt at such length on the assumption of this primitive condition, it is because, having ancient errors and inveterate prejudices to destroy, I thought I ought to dig down to the root and show, in the panorama of the true state of nature, how far even natural inequality is from having as much reality and influence in that state as our writers claim.

In fact, it is easy to see that, among the differences that distinguish men, some pass for natural that are uniquely the work of habit and the various types of life men adopt in society. Thus a robust or delicate temperament, and the strength or weakness that depend on it, often come more from the harsh or effeminate way in which one has been raised than from the primitive constitution of bodies. The same is true of strengths of mind; and not only does education establish a difference between cultivated minds and those that are not, but it augments the difference among the former in proportion to their culture; for should a giant and a dwarf walk on the same road, every step they both take will give fresh advantage to the giant. Now if one compares the prodigious diversity of educations and types of life that prevails in the different orders of the civil state with the simplicity and uniformity of animal and savage life, in which all nourish themselves on the same foods, live in the same manner, and do exactly the same things, it will be understood how much less the difference between one man and another must be in the state of nature than in society, and how much natural inequality must increase in the human species through instituted inequality.

But even if nature displayed as much partiality in the distribution of its gifts as is claimed, what advantage would the most favored draw from them to the prejudice of others in a state of things that allowed for almost no relations of any sort between them? Where there is no love, of what use is beauty? What is the use of wit for people who do not speak, and ruse for those who have no dealings with one another? I hear it always repeated that the stronger will oppress the weak; but let someone explain to me what is meant by this word *oppression*. Some will dominate by violence, the others will groan, subjected to all of their whims. That is precisely what I observe among us; but I do not see how the same could be said of savage men, whom it would even be rather difficult to get to understand what servitude and domination are. A man might well seize the fruits another has gathered, the game he has killed, the cave that served as his shelter; but how will he ever succeed in making himself obeyed, and what would be the chains of dependence among men who possess nothing? If someone chases me from a tree, I am at liberty to go to another; if someone torments me in one place, who will prevent me from going somewhere else? Is there a man whose strength is sufficiently superior to mine and who is, in addition, depraved enough, lazy enough, and wild enough to force me to provide for his subsistence while he remains idle? He must resolve not to lose sight of me for a single moment and to keep me very carefully tied up during his sleep, for fear that I should escape or kill him—that is to say, he is obliged to expose himself voluntarily to much greater trouble than he wants to avoid and gives to me. After all that, should his vigilance relax for a moment, should an unforeseen noise make him turn his head, I take twenty steps in the forest, my chains are broken, and he never in his life sees me again.

Without uselessly prolonging these details, everyone must see that, since the bonds of servitude are formed only from the mutual dependence of men and the reciprocal needs that unite them, it is impossible to enslave a man without first putting him in the position of being unable to do without another; a situation which, as it did not exist in the state of nature, leaves each man there free of the yoke, and renders vain the law of the stronger.

After having proved that inequality is barely perceptible in the state of nature, and that its influence there is almost nil, it remains for me to show its origin and progress in the successive developments of the human mind. After having shown that *perfectibility*, the social virtues, and the other faculties that natural man had received in potentiality, could never develop by themselves, that in order to develop, they needed the chance combination of several foreign causes which might never have arisen and without which he would have remained eternally in his primitive condition, it remains for me to consider and bring together the different accidents that were able to perfect human reason while deteriorating the species, make a being bad while making him sociable, and from such a distant origin finally bring man and the world to the point where we see them.

I admit that since the events I have to describe could have happened in several ways, I can make a choice only by conjectures. But besides the fact that these conjectures become reasons when they are the most probable that one can draw from the nature of things, and the sole means that one can have to discover the truth, the conclusions I want to deduce from mine will not thereby be conjectural, since, on the principles I have established, one could not conceive of any other system that would not provide me with the same results, and from which I could not draw the same conclusions.

This will exempt me from expanding my reflections on the way in which the lapse of time compensates for the slight probability of events; on the surprising power of very trivial causes when they act without interruption; on the impossibility, on the one hand, for one to destroy certain hypotheses, although on the other one cannot give them the degree of certainty of facts; on how, when two facts given as real are to be connected by a series of intermediate facts which are unknown or considered as such, it is up to history, when it exists, to present the facts that connect them; while it is up to philosophy, when history is lacking, to determine similar facts that might connect them; finally, on how, with reference to events, similarity reduces the facts to a much smaller number of different classes than is imagined. It is enough for me to offer these objects to the consideration of my judges; it is enough for me to have arranged it so that common readers would have no need to consider them.

Second Part

The first person who, having enclosed a plot of land, took it upon himself to say *this is mine*, and found people simple enough to believe him, was the true founder of civil society. What crimes, wars, murders, what miseries and horrors would humankind have been spared, by someone who, pulling up the stakes or filling in the ditch, had cried out to his fellow men: "Beware not to listen to this imposter. You are lost if you forget that the fruits of the earth belong to all and the earth to no one!" But it is very likely that by then things had already reached a point where they could no longer remain as they were. For this idea of property, depending on many prior ideas which could only have arisen successively, was not formed all at once in the human mind. Quite some progress had to have been made, industry and enlightenment acquired, transmitted, and augmented from age to age, before this last stage of the state of nature was reached. Let us therefore start further back in time and try to assemble from a single point of view this slow succession of events and advances in knowledge in their most natural order.

Man's first sentiment was that of his existence, his first care that of his preservation. The products of the earth provided him with all the necessary help; instinct led him to make use of them. Hunger and other appetites caused him to experience by turns various ways of existing, one of which invited him to perpetuate his species; and this blind inclination, devoid of any sentiment of the heart, produced only a purely animal act. The need satisfied, the two sexes no longer recognized one another, and even the child meant nothing to the mother once he could do without her.

Such was the condition of nascent man; such was the life of an animal at first limited to pure sensations, and scarcely profiting from the gifts nature offered him, let alone dreaming of wresting anything from it. But difficulties soon presented themselves; it was necessary to learn to vanquish them. The height of trees, which prevented him from reaching their fruits, competition from animals seeking to nourish themselves on these fruits, the ferocity of the animals that threatened his very life,

70

everything obliged him to apply himself to bodily exercises. He had to become agile, quick-footed, and vigorous in combat. Natural weapons, in the form of branches and stones, were soon found ready at hand. He learned to overcome nature's obstacles, combat other animals when necessary, fight for his subsistence even with men, or compensate for what had to be yielded to the stronger.

In proportion as humankind spread out, difficulties multiplied along with men. Differences of terrain, climate, and seasons could have forced them to introduce differences in their ways of life. Barren years, long and hard winters, scorching all-consuming summers, required new industry on their part. Along the seashores and riverbanks they invented line and hook, and became fishermen and fish eaters. In the forests they made bows and arrows, and became hunters and warriors. In cold countries they covered themselves with the skins of the animals they had killed. Lightning, a volcano, or some happy accident introduced them to fire, a new resource against the rigor of winter. They learned to preserve this element, then to reproduce it, and finally to prepare with it meats they previously devoured raw.

This repeated utilization of various beings in relation to himself, and of some beings in relation to others, must naturally have engendered in man's mind perceptions of certain relationships. These relations that we express by the words *large, small, strong, weak, fast, slow, fearful, bold*, and other similar ideas, compared when necessary and almost without thinking about it, finally produced in him some sort of reflection, or rather a mechanical prudence that indicated to him the precautions most necessary for his safety.

The new enlightenment that resulted from this development increased his superiority over the other animals by making him aware of it. He trained himself in setting traps for them; he tricked them in a thousand ways; and although several surpassed him in strength at fighting, or in speed at running, of those that might serve him or hurt him he became with time the master of the former, and the scourge of the latter. That is how his first glance at himself produced in him the first stirring of pride; that is how, while he was as yet scarcely able to distinguish ranks, and thought himself in the first rank by virtue of his species, he was preparing himself from afar to claim first rank as an individual.

Although his fellow men were not for him what they are for us, and although he hardly had more dealings with them than with other animals, they were not forgotten in his observations. The conformities that time could make him perceive among them, his female, and himself, led him to judge those he did not perceive; and seeing that they all behaved as he would have done under similar circumstances, he concluded that their way of thinking and feeling conformed entirely to his own. And this important truth, well established in his mind, made him follow, by a premonition as sure as dialectic[41] and more prompt, the best rules of conduct that it was suitable to observe toward them for his advantage and safety.

Taught by experience that love of well-being is the sole spring of human actions, he found himself able to distinguish the rare occasions when common interest should make him count on the assistance of his fellow men, and those even rarer occasions when competition should make him distrust them. In the first case, he united with them in a herd, or at most by some kind of free association that obligated no one and lasted only as long as the passing need that had formed it. In the second case, everyone sought to obtain his own advantage, either by overt force if he believed he could, or by cleverness and cunning if he felt himself to be the weaker.

This is how men could imperceptibly acquire some crude idea of mutual engagements and of the advantages of fulfilling them, but only insofar as present and perceptible interest could require; for foresight was nothing to them, and far from being concerned about a distant future, they did not even think of the next day. If a deer was to be caught, everyone clearly felt that for this purpose he ought faithfully to keep his post; but if a hare happened to pass within reach of one of them, there can be no doubt that he would have pursued it without scruple, and that having obtained his prey, he would have cared very little about having caused his companions to miss theirs.

It is easy to understand that such dealings did not require a language much more refined than that of crows or monkeys, which group together in about the same way. For a long time inarticulate cries, many gestures, and some imitative noises must have composed the universal language; by joining to this in each country a few articulated and conventional sounds—the institution of which, as I have already said, is not too easy to explain—there were individual languages, but crude and imperfect ones, approximately like those which various savage nations still have today. I cover multitudes of centuries in a flash, forced by time elapsing, the abundance of things I have to say, and the almost imperceptible progress of the beginnings; for the more slowly events succeeded one another, the more quickly can they be described.

[41] Dialectic is a form of argument.

These first advances finally put man in a position to make more rapid ones. The more the mind became enlightened, the more industry was perfected. Soon, ceasing to fall asleep under the first tree or to withdraw into caves, they discovered some kinds of hatchets of hard, sharp stones, which served to cut wood, dig the earth, and make huts from branches which they later decided to coat with clay and mud. This was the epoch of a first revolution, which produced the establishment and differentiation of families, and introduced a sort of property—from which perhaps many quarrels and fights already arose. However, since the strongest were probably the first to make themselves lodgings they felt capable of defending, it seems plausible that the weak found it quicker and safer to imitate them than to try to dislodge them; and as for those who already had huts, each man must seldom have sought to appropriate his neighbor's, less because it did not belong to him than because it was of no use to him, and because he could not seize it without exposing himself to a very lively fight with the family that occupied it.

The first developments of the heart were the effect of a new situation, that united husbands and wives, fathers and children in a common dwelling. The habit of living together gave rise to the sweetest sentiments known to men: conjugal love and paternal love. Each family became a little society all the better united because reciprocal affection and freedom were its only bonds; and it was then that the first difference was established in the ways of life of the two sexes, which until then had had but one. Women became more sedentary and grew accustomed to tending to the hut and the children, while the men went to seek their common subsistence. The two sexes also began, by a slightly softer life, to lose something of their ferocity and vigor. But if each person separately became less suited to combat savage beasts, on the contrary it was easier to assemble in order to resist them in common.

In this new state, with a simple and solitary life, very limited needs, and the implements they had invented to provide for them, since men enjoyed a great deal of leisure time, they used it to procure for themselves many kinds of commodities unknown to their fathers; and that was the first yoke they imposed on themselves without thinking about it, and the first source of the evils they prepared for their descendants. For, besides their continuing thus to soften body and mind, as these commodities had lost almost all their pleasantness through habit, and as they had at the same time degenerated into true needs, being deprived of them became much more cruel than possessing them was sweet; and people were unhappy to lose them without being happy to possess them.

Here one gets a somewhat better glimpse of how the use of speech was established or perfected imperceptibly in the bosom of each family; and one can further conjecture how various particular causes could have spread language and accelerated its progress by making it more necessary. Great floods or earthquakes surrounded inhabited areas with water or precipices; revolutions of the globe detached and broke up portions of the continent into islands. One can imagine that among men thus brought together and forced to live together, a common idiom must have been formed sooner than among those who wandered freely in the forests on the mainland. Thus it is very possible that after their first attempts at navigation, islanders brought the use of speech to us; and it is at least very probable that society and languages came into being on islands and were perfected there before they were known on the continent.

Everything begins to change its appearance. Men who until now had wandered in the woods, having become more settled, slowly come together, unite into different bands, and finally form in each country a particular nation, unified by customs and character, not by regulations and laws but by the same kind of life and foods and by the common influence of climate. A permanent proximity cannot fail finally to engender some contact between different families. Young people of different sexes live in neighboring huts; the passing dealings demanded by nature soon lead to another kind no less sweet and more permanent through mutual frequentation. People grow accustomed to consider different objects and to make comparisons; imperceptibly they acquire ideas of merit and beauty, which produce sentiments of preference. By dint of seeing one another, they can no longer do without seeing one another again. A tender and gentle sentiment insinuates itself into the soul and at the least obstacle becomes an impetuous fury. Jealousy awakens with love; discord triumphs, and the gentlest of the passions receives sacrifices of human blood.

As ideas and sentiments succeed one another, as the mind and the heart are trained, humankind continues to be tamed, relationships spread, and bonds tighten. People grew accustomed to assembling in front of the huts or around a large tree; song and dance, true children of love and leisure, became the amusement or rather the occupation of idle and assembled men and women. Each one began to look at the others and to want to be looked at himself, and public esteem acquired a value. The one who sang or danced best, the handsomest, the strongest, the most adroit, or the most eloquent became the most highly regarded; and this was the first step toward inequality and, at the same time, toward vice.

From these first preferences were born on the one hand vanity and contempt, on the other shame and envy; and the fermentation caused by
these new leavens eventually produced compounds fatal to happiness
and innocence.

As soon as men had begun to appreciate one another, and the idea
of regard took shape in their minds, each one claimed a right to it, and
no one could with impunity fail to show it toward anyone. From this
came the first duties of civility, even among savages; and from this any
voluntary wrong became an outrage, because along with the harm that
resulted from the injury, the offended party saw in it contempt for his
person, often more unbearable than the harm itself. Thus, everyone
punishing the contempt shown him in a manner proportionate to the
importance he accorded himself, vengeances became terrible, and men
bloodthirsty and cruel. This is precisely the stage reached by most of
the savage peoples known to us, and it is for want of having sufficiently
distinguished between ideas and noticed how far these peoples already
were from the first state of nature, that many have hastened to conclude
that man is naturally cruel, and that he needs civilization in order to
make him gentler; whereas, nothing is as gentle as man in his primitive
state when, placed by nature at equal distances from the stupidity of
brutes and the fatal enlightenment of civil man, and limited equally by
instinct and reason to protecting himself from the harm that threatens
him, he is restrained by natural pity from himself doing anyone harm,
and nothing leads him to do so even after harm has been done him. For,
according to the axiom of the wise Locke, *where there is no property,
there is no injury.*[42]

But it must be noted that society in its beginning stages and the relations already established among men required in them qualities different from those they derived from their primitive constitution; that,
since morality was beginning to be introduced into human actions, and
since, before there were laws, everyone was sole judge and avenger of
the offenses he had received, the goodness suited to the pure state of
nature was no longer that which suited nascent society; that punishments had to become more severe as the occasions for offense became
more frequent; and that it was up to the terror of revenge to take the
place of the restraint of laws. Thus, although men had come to have
less endurance, and although natural pity had already undergone some
alteration, this period in the development of human faculties, occupying

---

[42] Rousseau is citing the English political thinker John Locke (1632–1704), although
he misquotes him slightly. In his *Essay Concerning Human Understanding* IV, II, 18,
Locke writes, "Where there is no property, there is no injustice."

a middle position between the indolence of the primitive state and the petulant activity of our *amour propre*, must have been the happiest and most durable epoch. The more one reflects on it, the more one finds that this state was the least subject to revolutions, the best for man (XVI), and that he must have left it only by some fatal accident, which, for the sake of the common utility, ought never to have happened. The example of savages, almost all of whom have been found at this stage, seems to confirm that humankind was made to remain in it always; that this state is the veritable youth of the world; and that all subsequent progress has been in appearance so many steps toward the perfection of the individual, and in fact toward the decrepitude of the species.

As long as men were content with their rustic huts, as long as they limited themselves to sewing their clothing of skins with thorns or fish bones, adorning themselves with feathers and shells, painting their bodies different colors, perfecting or embellishing their bows and arrows, carving a few fishing canoes or a few crude musical instruments with sharp stones; in a word, as long as they applied themselves only to tasks that a single person could do and to arts that did not require the collaboration of several hands, they lived free, healthy, good, and happy insofar as they could be according to their nature, and they continued to enjoy among themselves the sweetness of independent exchange. But from the moment one man needed the help of another, as soon as it was thought to be useful for a single person to have provisions for two, equality disappeared, property was introduced, labor became necessary; and vast forests were changed into smiling fields which had to be watered with the sweat of men, and in which slavery and misery were soon seen to germinate and grow with the crops.

Metallurgy and agriculture were the two arts whose invention produced this great revolution. For the poet it is gold and silver, but for the philosopher it is iron and wheat that have civilized men and ruined humankind. And they were both unknown to the savages of America, who therefore have always remained such; other peoples seem even to have remained barbarians as long as they practiced one of these arts without the other. And perhaps one of the best reasons why Europe has been, if not earlier, at least more constantly and better civilized than the other parts of the world is that it is at the same time the most abundant in iron and the most fertile in wheat.

It is very difficult to conjecture how men came to know and use iron; for it is not plausible that they on their own thought of drawing the raw material from the mine and giving it the necessary preparations to make it fuse before they knew what would result. On the other hand, it is even harder to attribute this discovery to some accidental fire, because mines are formed only in arid spots, stripped of both trees and plants; so that one could say that nature had taken precautions to hide this deadly secret from us. There only remains, therefore, the extraordinary circumstance of some volcano that, by throwing up metallic materials in fusion, would have given observers the idea of imitating this operation of nature. Even then, they must be assumed to have had a good deal of courage and foresight to undertake such difficult labor and to envisage so far in advance the advantages they could draw from it: all of which hardly suits minds that are not already more trained than theirs must have been.

As for agriculture, its principle was known long before its practice was established, and it is hardly possible that men, constantly occupied with obtaining their subsistence from trees and plants, did not rather promptly have an idea of the ways used by nature to grow plants. But their industry probably turned in that direction only very late, either because trees, which along with hunting and fishing provided their food, did not need their care; or for want of knowing how to use wheat; or for want of implements with which to cultivate it; or for want of foresight concerning future need; or, finally, for want of means to prevent others from appropriating the fruit of their labor. Once they became industrious, it is credible that, with sharp stones and pointed sticks, they began by cultivating a few vegetables or roots around their huts long before they knew how to prepare wheat and had the implements necessary for large-scale cultivation. Besides, to devote oneself to that occupation and sow the land, one must be resolved to lose something at first in order to gain a great deal later: a precaution very far from the mind of savage man, who, as I have said, has a great deal of difficulty thinking in the morning of his needs for the evening.

The invention of the other arts was therefore necessary to force humankind to apply itself to that of agriculture. As soon as men were needed to smelt and forge iron, other men were needed to feed them. The more the number of workers was multiplied, the fewer hands there were furnishing the common subsistence, without there being fewer mouths to consume it; and since some needed foodstuffs in exchange for their iron, the others finally found the secret of using iron in order to multiply foodstuffs. From this arose farming and agriculture on the one hand, and the art of working metals and multiplying their uses on the other.

From the cultivation of land there necessarily followed its division; and from the property once recognized, the first rules of justice. For in order to give everyone what is his, it must be possible for each person to have something; moreover, as men began to look to the future and as they all saw themselves as having some goods to lose, there was not one of them who did not have to fear reprisals against himself for wrongs he might do to another. This origin is all the more natural as it is impossible to conceive of the idea of property arising from anything except manual labor; because one cannot see what man can add, other than his own labor, in order to appropriate things he has not made. It is labor alone which, giving the cultivator a right to the product of the land he has tilled, gives him a right to the soil as a consequence, at least until the harvest, and thus from year to year; which, creating continuous possession, is easily transformed into property.[43] When the Ancients, says Grotius, gave Ceres the title legislatrix,[44] and gave the name Thesmophoria to a festival celebrated in her honor, they thereby made it understood that the division of lands produced a new kind of right: that is, the right of property, different from the one that results from natural law.

Things in this state could have remained equal if talents had been equal, and if, for example, the use of iron and the consumption of foodstuffs had always been exactly balanced. But this proportion, which nothing maintained, was soon broken; the stronger did more work; the cleverer turned his to better advantage; the more ingenious found ways to shorten his labor; the farmer had a greater need of iron or the blacksmith a greater need of wheat; and working equally, the one earned a great deal while the other barely had enough to live. Thus does natural inequality imperceptibly manifest itself along with the inequality of combination, and thus do differences among men, developed by those of circumstances, become more perceptible, more permanent in their effects, and begin to influence the fate of individuals in the same proportion.

Things having reached this point, it is easy to imagine the rest. I will not stop to describe the successive invention of the other arts, the progress of languages, the testing and use of talents, the inequality of fortunes, the use or abuse of wealth, nor all the details that follow these, and that everyone can easily supply. I shall simply limit myself to a brief glance at humankind placed in this new order of things.

Behold all our faculties developed, memory and imagination in play, *amour propre* aroused, reason rendered active, and the mind having almost reached the limit of the perfection of which it is capable. Behold all the natural qualities put into action, the rank and fate of each man

---

[43] See Locke, Document 4.
[44] In Roman mythology, Ceres was the goddess of agriculture, especially corn. A legislatrix is a woman who makes laws.

established, not only upon the quantity of goods and the power to serve or harm, but also upon the mind, beauty, strength, or skill, upon merit or talents. And since these qualities are the only ones which could attract regard, one soon had to have them or to affect to have them; for one's own advantage, one had to appear to be other than what one in fact was. To be and to seem became two altogether different things; and from this distinction arose conspicuous ostentation, deceptive cunning, and all the vices that follow from them. From another point of view, man, having formerly been free and independent, is now subjected, so to speak, by a multitude of new needs to all of nature and especially to his fellow men, whose slave he in a sense becomes even in becoming their master; rich, he needs their services; poor, he needs their help; and mediocrity cannot enable him to do without them. He must therefore incessantly seek to interest them in his fate, and to make them find their own profit, in fact or in appearance, in working for his. This makes him deceitful and crafty with some, imperious and harsh with others, and makes it necessary for him to abuse all those whom he needs when he cannot make them fear him and does not find it in his interest to serve them usefully. Finally, consuming ambition, the fervor to raise one's relative fortune less out of true need than in order to place oneself above others, inspires in all men a base inclination to harm each other, a secret jealousy all the more dangerous because, in order to strike its blow in greater safety, it often assumes the mask of benevolence: in a word, competition and rivalry on one hand, opposition of interest on the other, and always the hidden desire to profit at the expense of others. All these evils are the first effect of property and the inseparable consequence of nascent inequality.

Before representative signs of wealth had been invented, it could hardly consist in anything except land and livestock, the only real goods men can possess. Now, once inheritances had increased in number and size to the point of covering the entire earth and of all bordering on each other, some of them could no longer be enlarged except at the expense of others; and the supernumeraries, whom weakness or indolence had prevented from acquiring an inheritance in their turn, having become poor without having lost anything, because while everything around them changed they alone had not changed at all, were obliged to receive or steal their subsistence from the hands of the rich; and from that began to arise, according to the diverse characters of the rich and the poor, domination and servitude or violence and plunder. The rich, for their part, had scarcely known the pleasure of domination when they soon disdained all others, and using their old slaves to subdue new ones, they thought only of subjugating and enslaving their neighbors: like those famished wolves which, having once tasted human flesh, reject all other food and thenceforth want only to devour men. Thus, while the most powerful or most miserable claimed on the basis of their strength or of their needs a sort of right to the goods of others, equivalent, according to them, to the right of property, the breakdown of equality was followed by the most frightful disorder; thus the usurpations of the rich, the banditry of the poor, the unbridled passions of all, stifling natural pity and the as yet weak voice of justice, made man avaricious, ambitious, and evil. Between the right of the stronger and the right of the first occupant there arose a perpetual conflict, which ended only in fights and murders (XVII). Nascent society gave way to the most horrible state of war: Humankind, debased and devastated, no longer able to turn back or renounce the unhappy acquisitions it had made, and working only toward its shame by abusing the faculties that honor it, brought itself to the brink of its ruin.

Attonitus novitate mali, divesque miserque,
Effugere optat opes, et quae modo voverat, odit[45]

It is not possible that men should not at last have reflected upon such a miserable situation and upon the calamities besetting them. The rich, above all, must have soon felt how disadvantageous to them was a perpetual war in which they alone paid all the costs, and in which the risk of life was common to all while the risk of goods was personal. Moreover, in whatever light they presented their usurpations, they felt strongly enough that these were established only on a precarious and abusive right, and that having been acquired only by force, force could take them away without their having any reason to complain. Even those enriched by industry alone could hardly base their property upon better titles. In vain could they say: I built this wall; I earned this field by my labor. Who gave you its dimensions, they might be answered, and by virtue of what do you presume to be paid at our expense for work we did not impose on you? Do you not know that a multitude of your brothers perish or suffer from need of what you have in excess, and that you needed the express and unanimous consent of humankind in order to appropriate for yourself anything from the common subsistence that went beyond your

---

[45] "Shocked by the novelty of the evil, rich, and yet wretched, he seeks to run away from his wealth and hates what he once prayed for." Rousseau here cites Ovid (43 B.C.E.–17 or 18 C.E.), a Roman poet who wrote about love and mythological transformation. This is from *Metamorphoses* XI.

own? Destitute of valid reasons to justify himself and of sufficient forces to defend himself; easily crushing an individual, but himself crushed by groups of bandits; alone against all, and unable because of mutual jealousies to unite with his equals against enemies united by the common hope of plunder, the rich man, pressed by necessity, finally conceived the most calculated project that ever entered the human mind. It was to use in his favor the very forces of those who attacked him, to make his defenders out of his adversaries, inspire them with other maxims, and give them other institutions which were as favorable to him as natural right was against him.

To this end, after having shown his neighbors the horror of a situation that armed them all against each other, that made their possessions as burdensome as their needs, and in which no one found security in either poverty or wealth, he easily invented specious reasons to lead them to his goal. "Let us unite," he told them, "to protect the weak from oppression, restrain the ambitious, and secure for everyone the possession of what belongs to him. Let us institute regulations of justice and peace to which all are obliged to conform, which make an exception of no one, and which compensate in some way for the caprices of fortune by equally subjecting the powerful and weak to mutual duties. In a word, instead of turning our forces against ourselves, let us gather them into one supreme power which governs us according to wise laws, protects and defends all the members of the association, repulses common enemies, and maintains us in an eternal concord."

Far less than the equivalent of this discourse was necessary to sway crude, easily seduced men, who in addition had too many matters to straighten out among themselves to be able to do without arbiters, and too much avarice and ambition to be able to do without masters for long. All ran to meet their chains believing they secured their freedom, for although they had enough reason to feel the advantages of a political establishment, they did not have enough experience to foresee its dangers. Those most capable of anticipating the abuses were precisely those who counted on profiting from them; and even the wise saw the necessity of resolving to sacrifice one part of their freedom for the preservation of the other, just as a wounded man has his arm cut off to save the rest of his body.

Such was, or must have been, the origin of society and laws, which gave new fetters to the weak and new forces to the rich (XVIII), destroyed natural freedom for all time, established forever the law of property and inequality, changed a clever usurpation into an irrevocable right, and for the profit of a few ambitious men henceforth subjected the whole of humankind to work, servitude, and misery. It is easy to see how the establishment of a single society made that of all the others indispensable, and how, to stand up to united forces, it was necessary to unite in turn. Societies, multiplying or spreading rapidly, soon covered the entire surface of the earth; and it was no longer possible to find a single corner in the universe where one could free oneself from the yoke and withdraw one's head from the often ill-guided sword that every man saw perpetually hanging over his head. Civil right having thus become the common rule of citizens, the law of nature no longer operated except between the various societies, where, under the name law of nations, it was tempered by some tacit conventions in order to make commerce possible and to take the place of natural commiseration which, losing between one society and another nearly all the force it had between one man and another, no longer dwells in any but a few great cosmopolitan souls, who surmount the imaginary barriers that separate peoples and who, following the example of the sovereign being who created them, include the whole of humankind in their benevolence.

The bodies politic, thus remaining in the state of nature with relation to each other, soon experienced the inconveniences that had forced individuals to leave it; and among these great bodies that state became even more fatal than it had previously been among the individuals of whom they were composed. Hence arose the national wars, battles, murders, and reprisals that make nature tremble and shock reason, and all those horrible prejudices, which rank the honor of shedding human blood among the virtues. The most decent people learned to consider it one of their duties to murder their fellow men; finally, men were seen massacring each other by the thousands without knowing why; more murders were committed on a single day of combat and more horrors in the capture of a single city than were committed in the state of nature during whole centuries over the entire face of the earth. Such are the first effects one glimpses of the division of humankind into different societies. Let us return to their institution.

I know that many have attributed other origins to political societies, such as conquests by the more powerful, or union of the weak; and the choice among these causes is indifferent to what I want to establish. However, the one I have just presented appears to me the most natural for the following reasons. 1. In the first case, the right of conquest, as it is not a right, could not have founded any other, since the conqueror and the conquered peoples always remain in a state of war with each other, unless the nation, returned to complete freedom, should voluntarily choose its conqueror as its leader. Until then, whatever capitulations may have been made, since they were based only on violence and are consequently null by that very fact, there can, on this hypothesis, be neither true society nor body politic, nor any other law than that of the stronger. 2. In the second case, these words *strong* and *weak* are equivocal; because, in the interval between the establishment of the right of property or of the first occupant and that of political governments, the meaning of these terms is better expressed by the words *poor* and *rich*, since before the laws a man did not, in fact, have any other means of subjecting his equals than by attacking their goods or by giving them some of his. 3. The poor having nothing to lose except their freedom, it would have been great folly for them to give away voluntarily the sole good remaining to them, without gaining anything in the exchange; on the contrary, the rich being so to speak vulnerable in every part of their goods, it was much easier to do them harm; they consequently had more precautions to take in order to protect themselves; and finally it is reasonable to believe that a thing was invented by those to whom it is useful rather than by those whom it wrongs.

Nascent government did not have a constant and regular form. The lack of philosophy and experience allowed only present inconveniences to be perceived, and one thought of remedying others only as they presented themselves. Despite all the labors of the wisest legislators, the political state remained forever imperfect because it was almost the work of chance, and because, as having begun badly, time revealed its defects and suggested remedies but could never repair the vices of the constitution. People were constantly patching it up, instead of which they should have begun by winnowing the threshing floor[46] and setting aside all the old materials, as Lycurgus[47] did in Sparta, in order to raise a good edifice afterward. At first, society consisted only of some general conventions, which all individuals pledged to observe, and by which the community became the guarantor for each individual. Experience had to show how weak such a constitution was, and how easy it was for lawbreakers to avoid conviction or punishment for faults of which the public alone was to be witness and judge; the law had to be evaded in a thousand ways; inconveniences and disorders had to keep multiplying before men finally thought of confiding to private individuals the dangerous trust of public authority, and committed to magistrates the care of enforcing observance of the deliberations of the people. For to say

---

[46] "To winnow the threshing floor" is a biblical expression. It appears twice in the Bible, each time referring to John the Baptist's preparing people for baptism. See Matthew 3:12 and Luke 3:17.

[47] Lycurgus is the name of the legendary founder of Sparta.

that leaders were chosen before the confederation was created and that the ministers of laws existed before the laws themselves is a supposition that does not permit of serious debate.

It would be no more reasonable to believe that at first peoples threw themselves into the arms of an absolute master without conditions and for all time, and that the first means of providing for the common security imagined by proud and unconquered men was to rush into slavery. In fact, why did they give themselves superiors if not to defend themselves against oppression, and to protect their goods, their liberties, and their lives, which are, so to speak, the constituent elements of their being? Now, since in relations between one man and another, the worst that can happen to one is to see himself at the discretion of the other, would it not have been contrary to good sense to begin by surrendering into the hands of a leader the only things they needed his help to preserve? What equivalent could he have offered them for the concession of so fine a right? And had he dared to exact it under pretext of defending them, would he not immediately have received the answer of the allegory: What more will the enemy do to us? It is therefore incontestable, and it is the fundamental maxim of all political right, that peoples have given themselves leaders to defend their liberty and not to enslave themselves. *If we have a prince*, said Pliny to Trajan, *it is so that he may preserve us from having a master.*[48]

Our politicians propound the same sophisms about the love of liberty that our philosophers made about the state of nature; on the basis of the things they see, they judge of very different things which they have not seen, and they attribute to men a natural inclination to servitude because of the patience with which the men who are before their eyes bear their servitude, not realizing that it is as true of liberty as it is of innocence and virtue, that their value is felt only as long as one enjoys them oneself, and the taste for them is lost as soon as they are lost. I know the delights of your country, said Brasidas to a satrap who compared the life of Sparta to that of Persepolis;[49] but you cannot know the pleasures of mine.

As an untamed steed bristles its mane, stamps the ground with its hoof, and breaks away impetuously at the mere approach of the bit, while a trained horse patiently endures the whip and the spur, so barbarous man does not bend his head for the yoke that civilized man wears

---

[48] Pliny the Younger (62–113 C.E.) was a Roman statesman. Trajan (53–117 C.E.) was a Roman emperor.

[49] Brasidas (d. 422 B.C.E.) was a Spartan officer in the Peloponnesian War. A satrap was a Persian official, and Persepolis was an important city in the Persian Empire.

without a murmur, and he prefers the most turbulent freedom to tranquil subjection. Therefore it is not by the degradation of enslaved peoples that man's natural dispositions for or against servitude must be judged, but by the marvels done by all free peoples to guard themselves from oppression. I know that the former do nothing but boast incessantly of the peace and quiet they enjoy in their chains, and that *miserrimam servitutem pacem appellant.*[50] But when I see the others sacrifice pleasures, rest, wealth, power, and life itself for the preservation of this sole good which is so disdained by those who have lost it; when I see animals born free and abhorring captivity break their heads against the bars of their prison; when I see multitudes of entirely naked savages scorn European voluptuousness and brave hunger, fire, the sword, and death to preserve only their independence, I sense that it is not for slaves to reason about liberty.

As for paternal authority, from which many have derived absolute government and all society, without having recourse to the contrary proofs of Locke and Sidney,[51] it suffices to note that nothing in the world is farther from the ferocious spirit of despotism than the gentleness of that authority which looks more to the advantage of the one who obeys than to the utility of the one who commands; that by the law of nature, the father is master of the child only as long as his help is necessary for him; that beyond this stage they become equals, and the son, perfectly independent of the father, then owes him only respect and not obedience; for gratitude is certainly a duty that must be rendered, but not a right that can be required. Instead of saying that civil society is derived from paternal power, it should be said on the contrary that it is from civil society that this power draws its principal force. An individual was only recognized as the father of many when they remained assembled around him. The goods of the father, of which he is truly the master, are the bonds that keep his children dependent on him, and he can give them a share of his inheritance only in proportion as they shall have well deserved it from him by continual deference to his wishes. Now subjects, far from having some similar favor to expect from their despot, since they and all they possess belong to him as his own, or at least he claims this to be the case, are reduced to receiving as a favor whatever

---

[50] "They call the most miserable servitude peace." Tacitus's *Histories* were written in 109 C.E.

[51] The English politician and political theorist Algernon Sidney (ca. 1622–1683) was the author of *Discourses Concerning Government*, in which he argued against the patriarchalism of Robert Filmer (1588–1653) and the divine right of kings.

he leaves them of their own goods. He renders justice when he plunders them; he renders grace when he lets them live.

Continuing thus to test the facts by right, one would find no more solidity than truth in the voluntary establishment of tyranny; and it would be difficult to show the validity of a contract that obligated only one of the parties, in which one side granted everything and the other nothing, and which could only prove prejudicial to the one who commits himself. This odious system is very far from being, even today, that of wise and good monarchs, and especially of the kings of France, as may be seen in various parts of their edicts and particularly in the following passage of a famous text, published in 1667 in the name and by orders of Louis XIV: *Let it not be said therefore that the sovereign is not subject to the laws of his state, since the contrary proposition is a truth of the law of nations, which flattery has sometimes attacked, but which good princes have always defended as a tutelary divinity of their states. How much more legitimate is it to say with wise Plato, that the perfect felicity of a kingdom is that a prince be obeyed by his subjects, that the prince obey the law, and that the law be right and always directed to the public good.*[52] I will not stop to investigate whether, liberty being the most noble of man's faculties, it is not to degrade one's nature, to put oneself on the level of beasts enslaved by instinct, even to offend the author of one's being, to renounce without reservation the most precious of all his gifts and subject ourselves to committing all the crimes he forbids us in order to please a ferocious or insane master; nor whether that sublime workman ought to be more irritated at seeing his finest work destroyed than at seeing it dishonored. **I will ignore, if one wishes, the authority of Barbeyrac,[53] who flatly declares, following Locke, that no one may sell his liberty to the point of subjecting himself to an arbitrary power that treats him according to its fancy:** *Because,* **he adds,** *that would be selling one's own life, of which one is not the master.* I will only ask by what right those who were not afraid to debase themselves to this degree could subject their posterity to the same ignominy, and on its behalf renounce goods which it does not owe

---

[52] This curious passage comes from *Treatise on the Rights of the Very Christian Queen over Various States of the Monarchy of Spain* (1667). It suggests, ironically, that even Louis XIV believed that he was obliged to obey laws and that this was according to "the law of nations."

[53] Jean Barbeyrac (1674–1744) was a French jurist who translated into French the work of other important jurists who wrote on natural law and the social contract, such as Grotius and Pufendorf. Barbeyrac added important commentaries to their work, often inspired by Locke.

to their liberality and without which life itself is burdensome to all who are worthy of it?

Pufendorf says that just as one transfers one's goods to another by conventions and contracts, one can also divest oneself of one's freedom in favor of someone else. That, it seems to me, is very bad reasoning: For, in the first place, the goods I alienate become something altogether foreign to me, the abuse of which is indifferent to me; but it matters to me that my liberty is not abused, and I cannot, without making myself guilty of the evil I will be forced to do, expose myself to becoming the instrument of crime. Moreover, as the right of property is only conventional and of human institution, every man can dispose at will of what he possesses. But it is not the same for the essential gifts of nature, such as life and freedom, which everyone is permitted to enjoy and of which it is at least doubtful that one has the right to divest oneself: By giving up the one, one degrades one's being, by giving up the other, one destroys it insofar as one can; and as no temporal goods can compensate for the one or the other, it would offend both nature and reason to renounce them whatever the price. But if one could alienate one's freedom like one's goods, there would be a very great difference for children, who enjoy the father's goods only by transmission of his right; whereas since liberty is a gift they receive from nature by being men, their parents did not have any right to divest them of it. So that just as violence had to be done to nature to establish slavery, nature had to be changed to perpetuate this right. And the jurists, who have gravely pronounced that the child of a slave would be born a slave, have decided in other terms that a man would not be born a man.

It therefore seems certain to me not only that governments did not begin by arbitrary power, which is only their corruption and extreme limit, and which finally brings them back to the sole law of the strongest for which they were originally the remedy; but also that even if this is how they did begin, arbitrary power, being illegitimate by its nature, could not have served as a foundation for the rights of society, nor consequently for instituted inequality.

Without entering at present into the research yet to be undertaken on the nature of the fundamental compact of all government, I here limit myself, in following common opinion, to consider the establishment of the body politic as a true contract between the people and the leaders it chooses for itself: a contract by which the two parties obligate themselves to observe laws that are stipulated in it and that form the bonds of their union. The people having, in regard to social relations, united all their wills into a single one, all the articles on which this will expresses itself become so many fundamental laws obligating all members of the state without exception, and one of these laws regulates the choice and power of magistrates charged with watching over the execution of the others. This power extends to everything that can maintain the constitution, without going so far as to change it. To it are joined honors that render the laws and their ministers respectable and, for the latter personally, prerogatives that compensate them for the difficult labors that good administration requires. The magistrate, for his part, obligates himself to use the power confided in him only according to the intention of the constituents, to maintain each one in the peaceable enjoyment of what belongs to him, and to prefer on all occasions the public utility to his own interest.

Before experience had shown or knowledge of the human heart had made men foresee the inevitable abuses of such a constitution, it must have appeared all the better because those who were charged with watching over its preservation were themselves the most interested in it. For the magistracy and its rights being established only upon the fundamental laws, should they be destroyed the magistrates would immediately cease to be legitimate, the people would no longer be bound to obey them; and since it would have been the law and not the magistrate that constituted the essence of the state, everyone would return by right to his natural liberty.

If one only paused to reflect on it attentively, this would be confirmed by new reasons, and it would be evident from the nature of the contract that it could not be irrevocable: For if there were no superior power which could guarantee the fidelity of the contracting parties or force them to fulfill their reciprocal engagements, the parties would remain sole judges in their own case, and each would always have the right to renounce the contract as soon as he found either that the other had violated its terms, or that the conditions ceased to suit him. It is on this principle that the right to abdicate can, it seems, be based. Now to consider, as we are doing, only what is of human institution, if the magistrate, who has all the power in his hands and who appropriates for himself all the advantages of the contract, nevertheless had the right to renounce his authority, then there is all the more reason that the people, who pay for all the faults of the leaders, should have the right to renounce their dependence. But the frightful dissensions, the infinite disorders that this dangerous power would necessarily entail demonstrate more than anything else how much human governments needed a basis more solid than reason alone, and how necessary it was for public tranquility that divine will intervened to give sovereign authority a sacred and inviolable character that might deprive the subjects of the fatal right to dispose of it. If religion had accomplished only this good for men, it would be enough to oblige them all to cherish and adopt it, even with its abuses, since it spares even more blood than fanaticism causes to be shed. But let us follow the thread of our hypothesis.

The different forms of governments owe their origin to the greater or lesser differences that were found among individuals at the moment of institution. If one man was eminent in power, virtue, wealth, or credit, he alone was elected magistrate, and the state became monarchical. If several men approximately equal among themselves prevailed over all others, they were elected jointly and there was an aristocracy. Those whose fortune or talents were less disproportionate, and who were the least removed from the state of nature, kept the supreme administration in common and formed a democracy. Time confirmed which of these forms was the most advantageous for men. Some remained solely subject to laws, others were soon obeying masters. Citizens wanted only to keep their freedom; subjects thought only of depriving their neighbors of theirs, since they could not bear that others should enjoy a good which they no longer enjoyed themselves. In a word, on one side were wealth and conquests, and on the other happiness and virtue.

In these different governments, all magistracies were at first elective; and when wealth did not prevail, preference was accorded to merit, which confers a natural ascendancy, and to age, which confers experience in business and composure in deliberations. The elders of the Hebrews, the Gerontes[54] of Sparta, the Senate of Rome, and even the etymology of our word *seigneur*[55] show how much old age was respected in former times. The more elections fell upon men advanced in age, the more frequent they became and the more their difficulties were felt. Intrigues arose, factions were formed, parties grew bitter, civil wars flared up; finally the blood of citizens was sacrificed to the so-called happiness of the state, and people were on the verge of falling back into the anarchy of former times. The ambition of the foremost men profited from these circumstances to perpetuate their offices within their families; the people, already accustomed to dependence, tranquility, and the comforts of life, and already incapable of breaking their chains, consented to let their servitude increase in order to strengthen their tranquility. Thus it was that the leaders, having become hereditary, grew accustomed to regard their magistracy as a family possession, to regard themselves as

[54] *Gerontes* is a Greek word meaning "elders."
[55] *Seigneur* is the French word for "lord."

proprietors of the state, of which they were at first only the officers, to call their fellow citizens their slaves, to count them like cattle among the things that belonged to them, and to call themselves equals of the gods and kings of kings.

If we follow the progress of inequality through these different revolutions, we will find that the establishment of the law and of the right of property was its first stage, the institution of the magistracy the second, and the third and last was the changing of legitimate power into arbitrary power. So that the status of rich and poor was authorized by the first epoch, that of powerful and weak by the second, and by the third that of master and slave, which is the last degree of inequality and the limit to which all the others finally lead, until new revolutions either dissolve the government altogether or bring it closer to its legitimate institution.

In order to understand the necessity of this progress, one must consider less the motives for the establishment of the body politic than the form it assumes in execution and the inconveniences it brings about: For the same vices that make social institutions necessary make their abuse inevitable. And since—with the sole exception of Sparta, where the law attended principally to the education of children and where Lycurgus established *mœurs* which almost allowed him to dispense with adding laws—laws, in general less strong than passions, contain men without changing them, it would be easy to prove that any government that, without being corrupted or altered, always worked exactly according to the ends of its institution, would have been instituted unnecessarily, and that a country where no one eluded the laws and abused the magistracy would need neither magistracy nor laws.

Political distinctions necessarily bring about civil distinctions. Growing inequality between the people and its leaders soon makes itself felt among private individuals, where it is modified in a thousand ways according to passions, talents, and circumstances. The magistrate cannot usurp illegitimate power without creating clients to whom he is forced to yield some part of it. Besides, citizens let themselves be oppressed only insofar as they are carried away by blind ambition; and looking more below than above them, domination becomes dearer to them than independence, and they consent to wear chains in order to give them to others in turn. It is very difficult to reduce to obedience someone who does not seek to command; and the most adroit politician would never succeed in subjecting men who wanted only to be free. But inequality spreads without difficulty among ambitious and cowardly souls, always ready to run the risks of fortune, and to dominate or serve almost indifferently, according to whether it proves favorable or adverse to them. Thus there must have come a time when the eyes of the people were so dazzled that their leaders had only to say to the smallest of men: Be great, you and all your progeny; immediately he appeared great to everyone as well as in his own eyes, and his descendants were exalted even more in proportion to their distance from him. The more remote and uncertain the cause, the greater the effect; the more idlers could be counted as family, the more illustrious it became.

If this were the place to go into details, I could easily explain how, even without the involvement of government, inequality of credit and authority becomes inevitable between private individuals (XIX) as soon as, united in one society, they are forced to compare themselves to each other and to take into account differences they find in the continual use they have to make of one another. These differences are of several kinds; but in general, since wealth, nobility or rank, power, and personal merit are the principal distinctions by which people measure themselves in society, I would prove that the agreement or conflict of these various forces is the surest sign of a well or badly constituted state. I would show that of these four types of inequality, as personal qualities are the origin of all the others, wealth is the last to which they are reduced in the end because, being the most immediately useful to well-being and the easiest to transmit, it is easily used to buy all the rest: an observation which can permit a rather exact judgment of the extent to which each people is removed from its primitive institution, and of the distance it has traveled toward the extreme limit of corruption. I would note how much that universal desire for reputation, honors, and preferences, which devours us all, trains and compares talents and strengths; how much it excites and multiplies passions; and making all men competitors, rivals, or rather enemies, how many reverses, successes, and catastrophes of all kinds it causes daily by making so many contenders race the same course. I would show that it is to this ardor to be talked about, to this furor to distinguish oneself, which nearly always keeps us outside of ourselves, that we owe what is best and worst among men, our virtues and our vices, our sciences and our errors, our conquerors and our philosophers, that is to say, a multitude of bad things as against a small number of good ones. Finally, I would prove that if one sees a handful of powerful and rich men at the height of grandeur and fortune, while the crowd grovels in obscurity and misery, it is because the former prize the things they enjoy only insofar as the others are deprived of them; and because, without changing their status, they would cease to be happy if the people ceased to be miserable.

But these details alone would be the subject matter of a considerable work in which one would weigh the advantages and inconveniences of all governments relative to the rights of the state of nature, and where one would unmask all the different faces behind which inequality has appeared until the present and may appear in future centuries, according to the nature of these governments and the revolutions time will necessarily bring about in them. One would see the multitude oppressed from within as a consequence of the very precautions it had taken against that which menaced it from without; one would see oppression grow continually, without the oppressed ever being able to know what its limit would be, or what legitimate means would be left them to stop it; one would see the rights of citizens and national liberties die out little by little, and the protests of the weak treated as seditious murmurs; one would see politics limit to a mercenary portion of the people the honor of defending the common cause; from that one would see arise the necessity of taxes, the discouraged farmer abandoning his field, even during peacetime, and leaving his plow to buckle on the sword; one would see emerge the fatal and bizarre rules of the point of honor; one would see the defenders of the fatherland become, sooner or later, its enemies, incessantly holding the dagger over their fellow citizens, and there would come a time when one would hear them say to the oppressor of their country:

Pectore si fratris gladium juguloque parentis
Condere me jubeas, gravidaeque in viscera partu
Conjugis, invitâ peragam tamen ominia dextrâ.[56]

From the extreme inequality of conditions and fortunes, from the diversity of passions and talents, from useless arts, from pernicious arts, from frivolous sciences would come scores of prejudices equally contrary to reason, happiness, and virtue. One would see leaders foment all that can weaken assembled men by disuniting them; all that can give society an air of apparent concord while sowing a seed of real division; all that can inspire defiance and mutual hatred in different orders through the opposition of their rights and interests, and consequently fortify the power that contains them all.

It is from the bosom of this disorder and of these revolutions that despotism, by degrees raising its hideous head and devouring all it had seen to be good and healthy in all parts of the state, would finally succeed in

---

[56] "If you order me to plunge the sword into my brother's breast, or my father's throat, or even my pregnant wife's womb, I shall do so, though my right arm be unwilling." Rousseau is quoting the Roman poet Lucan (39–65 C.E.). This is from *Pharsalia* I.

trampling underfoot the laws and the people, and in establishing itself upon the ruins of the republic. The times that would precede this last change would be times of troubles and calamities, but in the end everything would be engulfed by the monster, and peoples would no longer have leaders or laws but only tyrants. From that moment also *mœurs* and virtue would cease to be in question; for wherever despotism reigns, *cui ex honesto nulla est spes,*[57] it tolerates no other master. As soon as it speaks, there is neither probity nor duty to consult, and the blindest obedience is the sole virtue that remains for slaves.

Here is the last stage of inequality, and the extreme point that closes the circle and touches the point from which we started. Here all individuals become equals again because they are nothing; and subjects no longer having any law except the will of the master, nor the master any other rule except his passions, the notions of good and the principles of justice vanish once again. Here everything is brought back to the sole law of the stronger, and consequently to a new state of nature different from the one with which we began, in that the one was the state of nature in its purity, and this last one is the fruit of an excess of corruption. Besides, there is so little difference between these two states, and the contract of government is so completely dissolved by despotism, that the despot is master only as long as he is the strongest, and as soon as he can be driven out, he cannot protest against violence. The uprising that ends by strangling or dethroning a sultan is as lawful an act as those by which he disposed, the day before, of the lives and goods of his subjects. Force alone maintained him, force alone overthrows him. Everything thus occurs according to the natural order; and whatever the outcome of these short and frequent revolutions may be, no one can complain of another's injustice, but only of his own imprudence or his misfortune.

In discovering and following thus the forgotten and lost routes that must have led man from the natural state to the civil state; in reestablishing, along with the intermediary positions I have just noted, those that the pressure of time has made me suppress or that imagination has not suggested to me, every attentive reader cannot fail to be struck by the immense space that separates these two states. It is in this slow succession of things that he will see the solution to an infinite number of problems of morals and politics which the philosophers cannot resolve. He will sense that, the humankind of one age not being the humankind

---

[57] This phrase ("in which there is no hope to be derived from an honorable deed") is a variation upon one found in Tacitus's *Annals* V.

of another, the reason why Diogenes[58] did not find a man was that he sought among his contemporaries the man of a time that no longer existed. Cato,[59] he will say, perished with Rome and liberty because he was out of place in his century; and the greatest of men only astonished the world, which he would have governed five hundred years earlier. In a word, he will explain how the soul and human passions, altering imperceptibly, change their nature so to speak; why our needs and our pleasures change their objects in the long run; why, original man vanishing by degrees, society no longer offers to the eyes of the wise man anything except an assemblage of artificial men and factitious passions which are the work of all these new relations and have no true foundation in nature. What reflection teaches us on this subject, observation confirms perfectly; savage man and civilized man differ so much in the bottom of their hearts and inclinations that what constitutes the supreme happiness of one would reduce the other to despair. The former breathes only tranquility and liberty; he wants only to live and remain idle; and even the perfect quietude of the stoic does not approach his profound indifference for all other objects. On the contrary, the citizen, always active, sweats, agitates himself, torments himself incessantly in order to seek still more laborious occupations; he works to death, he even rushes to it in order to get in condition to live, or renounces life in order to acquire immortality. He pays court to the great whom he hates, and to the rich whom he scorns. He spares nothing in order to obtain the honor of serving them; he proudly boasts of his baseness and their protection; and proud of his slavery, he speaks with disdain of those who do not have the honor of sharing it. What a sight the difficult and envied labors of a European minister are for a Carib! How many cruel deaths would that indolent savage not prefer to the horror of such a life, which often is not even sweetened by the pleasure of doing good. But in order to see the goal of so many cares, the words *power* and *reputation* would have to have a meaning in his mind; he would have to learn that there is a kind of men who set some store by the consideration of the rest of the universe and who know how to be happy and content with themselves on the testimony of others rather than on their own. Such is, in fact, the true cause of all these differences; the savage lives within himself; the sociable man, always outside of himself, knows how to live only in the opinion of others; and it is, so to speak, from their judgment alone that he draws the sentiment of his own existence. It is

[58] Diogenes (ca. 412–323 B.C.E.) was a Greek philosopher who reputedly walked through the streets in the daytime carrying a lamp, claiming to be looking for a good man.
[59] Cato (234–149 B.C.E.) was a Roman statesman known for his integrity.

not part of my subject to show how, from such a disposition, so much indifference for good and evil arises along with such fine discourses on ethics; how, everything being reduced to appearances, everything becomes factitious and deceptive: honor, friendship, virtue, and often even vices themselves, about which men finally discover the secret of boasting; how, in a word, always asking others what we are and never daring to question ourselves on this subject, in the midst of so much philosophy, humanity, politeness, and sublime maxims, we have only a deceitful and frivolous exterior, honor without virtue, reason without wisdom, and pleasure without happiness. It is sufficient for me to have proved that this is not the original state of man; and that it is the spirit of society alone, and the inequality it engenders, which thus change and alter all our natural inclinations.

I have tried to set forth the origin and progress of inequality, the establishment and abuse of political societies insofar as these things can be deduced from the nature of man by the light of reason alone, and independently of the sacred dogmas which give to sovereign authority the sanction of divine right. It follows from this exposition that inequality, being almost nonexistent in the state of nature, draws its force and growth from the development of our faculties and the progress of the human mind, and finally becomes stable and legitimate by the establishment of property and laws. It follows, further, that moral inequality, authorized by positive right alone, is contrary to natural right whenever it is not combined in the same proportion with physical inequality: a distinction which sufficiently determines what one ought to think in this regard of the sort of inequality that reigns among all civilized people; since it is manifestly against the law of nature, in whatever manner it is defined, that a child command an old man, an imbecile lead a wise man, and a handful of men be glutted with superfluities while the starving multitude lacks necessities.

[Notes]

I) Herodotus[60] relates that after the murder of the false Smerdis, when the seven liberators of Persia assembled to deliberate upon the form of government they would give the state, Otanes strongly favored a republic: an opinion all the more extraordinary in the mouth of a satrap in that, besides the claim he could have to the empire, grandees fear more than

---

[60] Herodotus (ca. 484–ca. 425 B.C.E.) was a Greek historian, widely regarded as "the father of history."

death a sort of government that forces them to respect men. Otanes, as may be expected, was not heeded; and seeing that they were going to proceed to the election of a monarch, he, who wanted neither to obey nor command, voluntarily yielded his right to the crown to the other contenders, asking as his only compensation that he and his posterity be free and independent. This was granted him. If Herodotus did not inform us of the restriction that was placed on this privilege, it would necessarily have to be assumed; otherwise Otanes, not recognizing any sort of law and not accountable to anyone, would have been all-powerful in the state and more powerful than the king himself. But it was scarcely likely that a man capable of contenting himself with such a privilege, in a case like this, was capable of abusing it. Indeed, there is no evidence that this right ever caused the least trouble in the kingdom, due either to the wise Otanes or to any one of his descendants.

II) From the outset I confidently rely on one of those authorities that are respectable to philosophers because they come from a solid and sublime reason which philosophers alone know how to find and appreciate. "Whatever interest we may have to know ourselves, I am not sure whether we do not know better everything that is not ourselves. Provided by nature with organs destined exclusively for our preservation, we use them only to receive foreign impressions, we seek only to extend beyond ourselves, and exist outside ourselves. Too busy multiplying the functions of our senses and augmenting the external range of our being, we rarely use that internal sense which reduces us to our true dimensions, and which separates from us all that is not part of us. However, this is the sense we must use if we wish to know ourselves; it is the only one by which we can judge ourselves. But how can this sense be made active and given its full range? How can we rid our soul, in which it resides, of all the illusions of our mind? We have lost the habit of using it, it has remained without exercise in the midst of the tumult of our bodily sensations, it has been dried out by the fire of our passions; heart, mind, senses, everything has worked against it." Hist[oire] Nat[urelle] T. 4, p. 151 de la Nat[ure] de l'homme.[61]

III) The changes that a long habit of walking on two feet could have produced in the conformation of man, the similarities that can still be observed between his arms and the forelegs of quadrupeds, and the

---

[61] George-Louis Leclerc de Buffon (1707–1788), France's foremost natural scientist, began publishing his monumental *Natural History* in 1749. See Document 5.

inference drawn from their way of walking, may have given rise to doubts about which way of walking must have been most natural for us. All children begin by walking on all fours and need our example and our lessons to learn to stand upright. There are even savage nations, such as the Hottentots, which greatly neglect their children and let them walk on their hands for so long that they then have great difficulty getting them to straighten up; the children of the Caribs of the Antilles do the same. There are various examples of quadruped men; and among others I could cite that of the child who was found in 1344 near Hesse, where he had been raised by wolves, and who said afterward at the court of Prince Henry that if it had been up to him, he would have preferred to return to them than to live among men. He had so thoroughly adopted the habit of walking like those animals that pieces of wood had to be tied to him which forced him to stand upright and keep his balance on his two feet. The same was true of the child found in 1694 in the forests of Lithuania, and who lived among bears. He gave no sign of reason, says M. de Condillac, walked on his hands and feet, had no language, and made sounds which in no way resembled those of a human being. The little savage of Hanover, who was brought to the court of England several years ago, had all the trouble in the world getting adjusted to walking on two feet; and in 1719 two more savages, found in the Pyrenees, roamed the mountains in the manner of quadrupeds. As for the objection one could make that this deprives man of the use of his hands, from which we derive so many advantages, besides the example of monkeys, which shows that the hand can very well be used in both ways, it would only prove that man can assign to his limbs a more convenient destination than that of nature, and not that nature destined man to walk otherwise than it teaches him to do.

But there are, it seems to me, much better reasons to support the claim that man is a biped. First, even if it were shown that he could have originally been formed otherwise than he visibly is, and nevertheless finally become what he is, this would not be enough to conclude that this is how it happened; for, besides showing that these changes are possible, it would still be necessary, before accepting them, at least to demonstrate their probability. Furthermore, while it does seem that man's arms could have served him for legs in case of need, this is the only observation that lends support to that system, as against a great number of others that are contrary to it. The principal ones are that the manner in which man's head is attached to his body, instead of directing his sight horizontally, as do all the other animals, and as he himself does when walking erect, would have kept him, while walking on all fours, with his eyes directly fastened on the ground, a situation but little favorable to the preservation of the individual; that the tail he lacks, and of which he has no need walking on two feet, is useful to quadrupeds, and none of them is deprived of one; that the breast of a woman, very well placed for a biped who holds her child in her arms, is so badly placed for a quadruped that none has it that way; that the rear quarters being of an excessive height in proportion to the forelegs, so that when walking on all fours we crawl on our knees, the whole would have been an animal ill proportioned and walking uncomfortably; that if he had set his foot down flat as well as the hand, he would have had one less articulation in the posterior leg than do other animals, namely the one that joins the canon bone to the tibia; and that setting down only the tip of the foot, as he doubtless would have been constrained to do, the tarsus, without speaking of the plurality of bones composing it, seems too large to take the place of the cannon bone, and its articulations with the metatarsus and the tibia too close together to give the human leg, in this position, the same flexibility as those of quadrupeds. Since the example of children is taken from an age when natural forces are not as yet developed nor the limbs strengthened it proves nothing whatsoever; and I might as well say that dogs are not destined to walk because they only crawl several weeks after their birth. Particular facts also have little force against the universal practice of all men, even of nations that, having had no communication with others, could not have imitated them in anything. A child abandoned in some forest before being able to walk, and raised by some beast, will have followed the example of its nurse by learning to walk like her; habit could have given it a dexterity it did not get from nature; and just as armless people succeed, by dint of training, in doing everything with their feet that we do with our hands, so will it finally have succeeded in using its hands as feet.

IV) Should there be among my readers so bad a physicist as to raise objections regarding this assumption of the natural fertility of the earth, I will answer him with the following passage:

"Since plants draw much more substance for their nourishment from the air and water than they do from the earth, it happens that when they decay they restore more to the earth than they took from it; besides, a forest regulates rainwaters by preventing evaporation. Thus, in a woods left untouched for a long time, the layer of earth which supports vegetation would increase considerably; but since animals restore less than they take from the earth, and since men consume enormous quantities of wood and plants for fire and other uses, it follows that the layer of vegetative earth in an inhabited country must always diminish and finally become like the terrain of Arabia Petrae,[62] and like that of so many other provinces of the Orient—which is in fact the oldest inhabited region, where only salt and sand are found. For the fixed salt of plants and animals remains, while all the other parts are volatilized." M. de Buffon, Hist[oire] Nat[urelle].

To this may be added the factual proof of the quantity of trees and plants of all kinds that covered almost all the deserted islands discovered in recent centuries, and of what history teaches us about the immense forests that had to be felled everywhere on earth as it was populated or civilized. On this subject I will further make the following three additional remarks. First, if there is a kind of vegetation that could compensate for the depletion of vegetable matter brought about by animals according to M. de Buffon's reasoning, then it is above all woods, the tops and leaves of which collect and absorb more water and moisture than do other plants. Second, destruction of the soil, that is to say, the loss of the substance suited to vegetation, must accelerate in proportion as the earth is more cultivated and as more industrious inhabitants consume in greater abundance its products of all kinds. My third and most important remark is that the fruits of trees furnish animals with a more abundant supply of food than can other forms of vegetation: an experiment I made myself, by comparing the products of two fields equal in size and quality, the one covered with chestnut trees and the other sown with wheat.

V) Among quadrupeds, the two most universal distinguishing features of the carnivorous species are derived from the shape of the teeth, and the conformation of the intestines. Animals that live only on vegetation all have flat teeth, like the horse, ox, sheep, hare; but carnivorous animals have pointed ones, like the cat, dog, wolf, fox. And as for the intestines, the frugivorous animals have some, such as the colon, that are not found in carnivorous animals. It therefore seems that man, having teeth and intestines like those of frugivorous animals, should naturally be placed in that class; and not only do anatomical observations confirm this opinion, but the great works of antiquity are also very favorable to it. "Dicaearchus," says Saint Jerome,[63] "relates in his books on Greek

---

[62] Arabia Petrae was a province of the Roman Empire.
[63] St. Jerome (348–420 C.E.) was a church father best known for his Latin translation of the Bible.

antiquities that under the reign of Saturn, when the earth was still fertile by itself, no man ate flesh, but that all lived on fruits and vegetables which grew naturally." (Lib. 2 Adv. Jovinian.) **This opinion can also be backed up by the reports of several modern travelers. François Corréal, among others, testifies that most of the inhabitants of the Lucayes whom the Spanish transported to the islands of Cuba, Santo Domingo, and elsewhere, died from having eaten flesh.** From this it may be seen that I neglect many favorable points I could exploit. For as prey is almost the unique subject of fighting among carnivorous animals, and as frugivorous ones live among themselves in continual peace, if the human species were of this latter kind, it is clear that it would have had much greater facility subsisting in the state of nature, and much less need and fewer occasions to leave it.

VI) All knowledge that requires reflection, all knowledge acquired only by the linking of ideas and perfected only successively, seems to be altogether beyond the reach of savage man for want of communication with his fellow men, that is to say, for want of the instrument used for that communication and of the needs that make it necessary. His knowledge and efforts are limited to jumping, running, fighting, throwing a stone, climbing a tree. But if he only does these things, in return he does them much better than we, who do not have the same need of them as has he; and since they depend solely on bodily exercise and cannot be communicated or improved from one individual to another, the first man could have been just as skilled at them as his last descendants.

The reports of travelers are full of examples of the strength and vigor of men in barbarous and savage nations; they praise their dexterity and nimbleness scarcely less; and since eyes alone are needed to observe these things, nothing prevents our giving credence to what eye witnesses certify about them. I draw some examples at random from the first books that come to hand.

"The Hottentots," says Kolben,[64] "understand fishing better than the Europeans of the Cape. They are equally skilled with net, hook, and spear, in coves as well as in rivers. They catch fish by hand no less skillfully. They are incomparably dexterous at swimming. Their manner of swimming has something surprising about it, that is altogether peculiar to them. They swim with their body upright and their hands stretched out of the water, so that they appear to be walking on land. In

[64] The German Peter Kolben was sent to the Cape of Good Hope in 1705 and wrote a book mainly about the Hottentots he found there.

the greatest agitation of the sea, when the waves form so many mountains, they somehow dance on the back of the waves, rising and falling like a piece of cork."

"The Hottentots," the same author further says, "have surprising dexterity at hunting, and the nimbleness of their running surpasses the imagination." He is amazed that they do not more often put their agility to bad use, which sometimes happens, however, as can be judged from the example he gives. "A Dutch sailor, disembarking at the Cape," he says, "engaged a Hottentot to follow him to the city with a roll of tobacco weighing about twenty pounds. When they were both at some distance from the crew, the Hottentot asked the sailor if he knew how to run. Run? answered the Dutchman; yes, very well. Let us see, replied the African; and fleeing with the tobacco, he disappeared almost immediately. The sailor, astounded by such marvelous speed, did not think of chasing him, and he never again saw either his tobacco or his porter.

"They have such quick sight and such a sure hand that Europeans cannot come close to them. At a hundred paces they will hit a mark the size of a halfpenny with a stone; and what is more astonishing, instead of fixing their eyes on the target, as we do, they make continuous movements and contortions. It seems that their stone is carried by an invisible hand."

Father du Tertre[65] says nearly the same things about the savages of the Antilles that have just been read concerning the Hottentots of the Cape of Good Hope. He praises above all their accuracy in shooting, with arrows, flying birds and swimming fish, which they then catch by diving. The savages of North America are no less famous for their strength and dexterity, and here is an example that will permit us to judge that of the Indians of South America.

In the year 1746, an Indian from Buenos Aires, having been condemned to the galleys at Cadiz, proposed to the governor that he redeem his freedom by risking his life at a public festival. He promised that by himself he would attack the fiercest bull with no other weapon in hand than a rope; that he would bring it to the ground, seize it with his rope by whatever part they would indicate, saddle it, bridle it, mount it, and so mounted, fight two other bulls of the fiercest kind to be let out of the Torillo; and that he would put them all to death, one after another, at the instant they would command him to do so, and without help from anyone. This was granted him. The Indian kept his word, and succeeded

[65]The Dominican Father du Tertre (1610–1687) visited the Antilles and wrote *Histoire générale des Isles de Saint Christophe* (Paris, 1654).

in everything he had promised. On the way in which he did it and on all the details of the fight, one can consult the first volume, in-12° of *Observations sur l'histoire naturelle* by M. Gautier, page 262, from which this fact is taken.

VII) "The length of the life of horses," says M. de Buffon, "as in all other species of animals, is proportionate to the length of time of their growth. Man, who takes fourteen years to grow, can live six or seven times as long, that is to say ninety or one hundred years; the horse, whose growth is completed in four years, can live six or seven times as long, that is to say twenty-five or thirty years. The examples that could be contrary to this rule are so rare that they should not even be considered as an exception from which conclusions can be drawn; and just as heavy horses reach their growth in less time than delicate horses, so they live less time, and are old from the age of fifteen."

VIII) I believe I see another difference between carnivorous and frugivorous animals which is still more general than the one I remarked upon in note (V), since this one extends to birds. This difference consists in the number of young, which never exceeds two in each litter for the species that live only on vegetables, and which ordinarily goes beyond this number for carnivorous animals. It is easy to know nature's design in this regard by the number of teats, which is only two in each female of the first species, like the mare, cow, goat, doe, ewe, etc., and which is always six or eight in other females, like the bitch, cat, wolf, tigress, etc. The hen, goose, duck, which are all carnivorous birds, as are the eagle, sparrow hawk, screech owl, also lay and hatch a large number of eggs, which never happens to the pigeon, turtledove, nor to birds that eat absolutely nothing except grain, which hardly ever lay and hatch more than two eggs at a time. The reason that can be given for this difference is that animals that live only on grasses and plants, remaining almost the entire day at pasture and being forced to spend much time nourishing themselves, could not be adequate to the nursing of several young; whereas carnivorous ones, since they take their meal almost in an instant, can more easily and more frequently return to their young and their hunting, and compensate for the waste of such a large quantity of milk. There would be many particular observations and reflections to make about all this, but this is not the place for them, and it is sufficient for me to have shown in this part the most general system of nature, a system which furnishes a new reason to withdraw man from the class of carnivorous animals and to place him among the frugivorous species.

IX) A famous author calculating the goods and evils of human life, and comparing the two sums, found that the latter greatly surpassed the former, and that all things considered life was a rather poor present to man. I am not surprised by his conclusion; he drew all his reasons from the constitution of civil man. If he had gone back to natural man, it can be judged that he would have found very different results; he would have perceived that man has hardly any evils other than those he has given himself, and that nature would have been justified. It is not without difficulty that we have succeeded in making ourselves so unhappy. When, on the one hand, one considers the vast labors of men, so many sciences investigated, so many arts invented, and so many forces employed, chasms filled, mountains razed, rocks broken, rivers made navigable, lands cleared, lakes dug out, swamps drained, enormous buildings raised upon the earth, the sea covered with ships and sailors; and when, on the other hand, one searches with a little meditation for the true advantages that have resulted from all this for the happiness of the human species, one cannot fail to be struck by the astounding disproportion prevailing between these things, and to deplore man's blindness, which, to feed his foolish pride and who knows what vain admiration for himself, makes him run feverishly after all the miseries of which he is susceptible, and which beneficent nature had taken care to keep from him.

Men are wicked; sad and continual experience spares the need for proof. However, man is naturally good; I believe I have demonstrated it. What then can have depraved him to this extent, if not the changes that have befallen his constitution, the progress he has made, and the knowledge he has acquired? Let human society be as highly admired as one wants; it is nonetheless true that it necessarily moves men to hate one another in proportion to the conflict of their interests, to render one another apparent services and in effect to do one another every imaginable harm. What is one to think of dealings in which every private person's reason dictates to him maxims directly contrary to those that public reason preaches to the body of society, and in which everyone profits from the misfortune of others? There is perhaps not a single well-to-do person whose death is not secretly hoped for by greedy heirs and often his own children; no ship at sea whose wreck would not be good news to some merchant; not a single firm that a dishonest debtor would not wish to see burned along with all the papers in it; not a single people that does not rejoice at the disasters of its neighbors. Thus do we find our advantage in what harms our fellow men, and someone's loss almost always creates another's prosperity. But what is still more dangerous is that public calamities are awaited and hoped for by a multitude of individuals. Some want illnesses, others death, others war, others famine. I have seen horrible men weep with sadness at the prospect of a fertile year; and the great and deadly fire of London, which cost the life or goods of so many unfortunates, perhaps made the fortune of more than ten thousand people. I know that Montaigne[66] blames the Athenian Demades[67] for having had a worker punished who, by selling coffins at a high price, gained a great deal from the death of citizens. But the reason Montaigne advances, that everyone would have to be punished, clearly confirms my own. Let us therefore look through our frivolous displays of good will, to what goes on at the recesses of our hearts, and let us reflect on what must be the state of things in which all men are forced to flatter and to destroy one another, and in which they are born enemies by duty and swindlers by interest. If I am answered that society is so constituted that each man gains by serving the others, I will reply that this would be very well, if he did not gain still more by harming them. There is no profit, however legitimate, that is not surpassed by one that can be made illegitimately, and the wrong done a neighbor is always more lucrative than any services. It therefore only remains a matter of finding ways to ensure one's impunity; and that is the end to which the powerful put all their strength and the weak all their cunning.

Savage man, when he has eaten, is at peace with all nature, and the friend of all his fellow men. If he must sometimes contend for his meal, he never comes to blows without first having compared the difficulty of winning with that of finding his subsistence elsewhere; and as pride is not involved in the fight, it is ended by a few blows; the victor eats, the vanquished goes off to seek his fortune, and all is pacified. But for man in society it is a different business altogether: First he must provide for necessities, then superfluities; next come delicacies, then immense wealth, and then subjects, and then slaves; he has not a moment of respite. What is most singular is that the less natural and urgent the needs, the more the passions increase, and, what is worse, so does the power to satisfy them; so that after long periods of prosperity, after having swallowed up many treasures and devastated many men, my hero will end up butchering everything until he is the sole master of the universe. Such, in brief, is the moral picture, if not of human life, at least of the secret aspirations of the heart of every civilized man.

Compare, without prejudices, the state of civil man with that of savage man, and determine if you can how many new gates, other than his

---

[66] Michel de Montaigne (1533–1592) was an important French writer.
[67] Demades (ca. 380–318 B.C.E.) was an Athenian orator.

wickedness, his needs, and his miseries, the former has opened to suffering and death. If you consider the mental anguish that consumes us, the violent passions that exhaust and desolate us, the excessive labors with which the poor are overburdened, the still more dangerous softness to which the rich abandon themselves, and which cause the former to die of their needs and the latter of their excesses; if you think of the monstrous mixtures of foods, their noxious seasonings, the spoiled foodstuffs, the adulterated drugs, the knavery of those who sell them, the errors of those who administer them, the poisonous containers in which they are prepared; if you take note of the epidemics engendered by the bad air among the multitudes of men gathered together, to the illnesses occasioned by the delicacy of our way of life, by the alternating movements from the interior of our houses into the fresh air, the use of garments put on or taken off with too little precaution, and all the cares that our excessive sensuality has turned into necessary habits, the neglect or privation of which then costs us our life or our health; if you take into account fires and earthquakes which, burning or destroying whole cities, cause their inhabitants to die by the thousands; in a word, if you unite the dangers that all these causes continually gather over our heads, you will sense how dearly nature makes us pay for the scorn we have shown for its lessons.

I will not repeat here what I have said elsewhere about war; but I wish that informed men wanted or dared, for once, to give the public the details of the horrors committed in armies by the suppliers of food and hospital entrepreneurs. One would see that their none too secret maneuvers, because of which the most brilliant armies dissolve into less than nothing, cause more soldiers to perish than are cut down by the enemy's sword. It is no less astonishing further to calculate the men swallowed up by the sea every year, by either hunger, or scurvy, or pirates, or fire, or shipwreck. It is clear that it is to established property, and consequently to society, that must also be attributed the assassinations, poisonings, highway robberies, and even the punishments of these crimes, punishments that are necessary to prevent greater evils, but which, costing the lives of two or more for the murder of one man, nevertheless actually double the loss to the human species. How many shameful ways there are to prevent the birth of men and trick nature; either by those brutal and depraved tastes that insult its most charming work, tastes that neither savages nor animals ever knew and that have arisen in civilized countries only from a corrupt imagination; or by those secret abortions, worthy fruits of debauchery and vicious honor; or by the exposure or murder of a multitude of infants, victims of the misery of their parents or the barbarous shame of their mothers; or, finally, by the mutilation of those unfortunates, for whom a part of their existence and all their posterity are sacrificed to vain songs or, worse yet, to the brutal jealousy of a few men: a mutilation which, in this last case, doubly outrages nature, both by the treatment given those who suffer it and by the use to which they are destined![68]

But are there not a thousand more frequent and even more dangerous cases when paternal rights openly offend humanity? How many talents are buried and inclinations forced by the imprudent constraint of fathers! How many who would have distinguished themselves if they had occupied a suitable position, die unhappy and dishonored in some other position for which they had no taste! How many happy but unequal marriages have been broken or disturbed, and how many chaste wives dishonored, by an order of conditions that is always in contradiction with that of nature! How many other bizarre unions formed by interest and disavowed by love and reason! How many even honest and virtuous spouses torture one another because of being ill-matched! How many young and unhappy victims of their parents' greed plunge into vice or spend their sad days in tears, and groan in indissoluble chains which the heart rejects and gold alone forged! Happy sometimes are those women whose courage and even virtue tear them from life before barbarous violence forces them into crime or despair. Forgive me, father and mother forever deserving of sorrow: I regretfully embitter your suffering; but may it serve as an eternal and terrible example to anyone who dares, in the very name of nature, to violate the most sacred of its rights!

If I have spoken only of those badly formed unions that are the product of our civilization, is it to be thought that those over which love and sympathy have presided are themselves without disadvantages? What would happen if I undertook to show the human species attacked at its very source, and even in the most sacred of all bonds, where one no longer dares to listen to nature until after consulting his fortune, and where, with civil disorder confusing virtues and vices, continence becomes a criminal precaution and the refusal to give life to one's fellow man an act of humanity? But without tearing off the

---

[68] Rousseau is referring to the practice of castrating young boys to produce beautiful singing voices.

veil that covers so many horrors, let us be content to indicate the evil for which others must provide the remedy.

Add to all this the many unhealthy trades that shorten lives or destroy the constitution, such as labor in mines, various preparations of metals and minerals, especially lead, copper, mercury, cobalt, arsenic, realgar; those other perilous trades that daily cost the lives of many workers, some of them roofers, others carpenters, others masons, others working in quarries; gather all these things together, I say, and one will be able to see in the establishment and perfection of societies the reasons for the diminution of the species observed by more than one philosopher.

Luxury, impossible to prevent among men greedy for their own comfort and the regard of others, soon completes the evil that societies began; and on the pretext of providing a livelihood for the poor, who should never have been made so in the first place, it impoverishes everyone else, and depopulates the state sooner or later.

Luxury is a remedy far worse than the evil it claims to cure; or rather it is itself the worst of all evils in any state whatever, whether large or small, and which, in order to feed the crowds of lackeys and miserable people it has created, crushes and ruins the farmer and the citizen, like those scorching south winds which, covering grass and greenery with all-devouring insects, deprive useful animals of their sustenance, and bring famine and death wherever they make themselves felt.

From society and the luxury it engenders arise the liberal and mechanical arts, commerce, letters, and all those useless things that cause industry to flourish, enrich, and ruin states. The reason for this deterioration is very simple. It is easy to see that, by its nature, agriculture must be the least lucrative of all the arts, because its product being of the most indispensable use to all men, its price must be in proportion to the abilities of the poorest. From the same principle can be drawn this rule in general, that the arts are lucrative in inverse ratio to their utility, and that the most necessary must in the end become the most neglected. From this one sees what must be thought of the true advantages of industry and of the real effect that results from its progress.

Such are the perceptible causes of all the miseries into which opulence finally precipitates the most admired nations. As industry and the arts spread and flourish, the scorned farmer, burdened by taxes needed to support luxury, and condemned to spend his life between labor and hunger, abandons his fields to go to the cities in search of the bread he ought to be bringing there. The more the stupid eyes of the people are struck with admiration by capital cities; the more one should groan at the sight of the abandoned countryside, fallow fields, and main routes overrun by unfortunate citizens who have become beggars or thieves, and destined to end their misery one day on the rack or on a dung heap. Thus it is that the state, enriching itself on the one hand, weakens and depopulates itself on the other, and that the most powerful monarchies, after much labor to become opulent and deserted, end up by becoming the prey of the poor nations that succumb to the deadly temptation to invade them, and that grow rich and weak in their turn, until they are themselves invaded and destroyed by others.

Let someone deign to explain to us for once what could have produced those hordes of barbarians who, for so many centuries, inundated Europe, Asia, and Africa? Was it to the industry of their arts, the wisdom of their laws, and the excellence of their civil order that they owed this prodigious population? Let our learned men have the goodness to tell us why, far from multiplying to such an extent, these ferocious and brutal men, lacking enlightenment, lacking restraint, lacking education, did not all murder one another at every moment over their pastures or hunting grounds? Let them explain to us how these miserable men could have been so bold as to look straight in the eye of such clever people as we ourselves were, with such fine military discipline, such fine codes, and such wise laws? And why, finally, after society was perfected in the countries of the north, and so many pains taken there to teach men their mutual duties and the art of living together agreeably and peaceably, nothing like the great numbers of men which it used to produce is seen to come from them? I rather fear that someone might finally think of answering me that all these great things, namely the arts, sciences, and laws, were very wisely invented by men as a salutary plague to prevent the excessive increase of the species, for fear that this world, which is destined for us, might finally become too small for its inhabitants.

What, then? Must we destroy societies, annihilate thine and mine, and return to live in forests with bears?[69] A conclusion in the manner of my adversaries, which I prefer to anticipate rather than leave them the shame of drawing it. Oh you, to whom the heavenly voice has not made itself heard and who recognize no other destination for your species than to end this brief life in peace; you who are able to leave behind in the cities your fatal acquisitions, your worried minds, your corrupted hearts, and your unbridled desires; reclaim, since it is up to you, your ancient and first innocence; go into the woods to lose sight and memory of the crimes of your contemporaries, and have no fear of debasing

---

[69] Here Rousseau anticipates the responses of his critics and clearly states that a return to the state of nature is not possible for modern man.

your species in renouncing its enlightenment in order to renounce its vices. As for men like me, whose passions have forever destroyed their original simplicity, who can no longer subsist on grass and nuts, nor do without laws and leaders; those who were honored in their first father with supernatural lessons; those who will see, in the intention of giving human actions a morality from the start which they would not have acquired for a long time, the reason for a precept indifferent in itself and inexplicable in any other system; those, in a word, who are convinced that the divine voice called the whole human race to the enlightenment and happiness of celestial intelligences: All those will endeavor, through the exercise of virtues they obligate themselves to practice while learning to know them, to deserve the eternal reward they ought to expect from them; they will respect the sacred bonds of the societies of which they are members; they will love their fellow men and will serve them with all their power; they will scrupulously obey the laws, and the men who are their authors and ministers; they will honor above all the good and wise princes who will know how to prevent, cure, or palliate that multitude of abuses and evils always ready to crush us; they will animate the zeal of these worthy leaders, by showing them without fear and flattery the greatness of their task and the rigor of their duty. But they will nonetheless scorn a constitution that can be maintained only with the help of so many respectable people, who are more often wished for than available, and from which, despite all their care, there always arise more real calamities than apparent advantages.

X) Of the men we know, either on our own, or from historians, or from travelers, some are black, others white, others red; some wear their hair long, others have nothing but curly wool; some are almost entirely covered with hair, others do not even have a beard. There have been, and there perhaps still are, nations of men of gigantic size; and apart from the fable of the Pygmies, which may well be only an exaggeration, it is known that the Laplanders, and above all the Greenlanders, are well below the average size of man. It is even claimed that there are whole peoples that have tails like quadrupeds. And without accepting in blind faith the reports of Herodotus and Ctesias,[70] one can at least draw from them this very likely opinion: If good observations had been possible in those ancient times when different peoples differed in their ways of life more than they do today, then one would also have noted much more

---

[70] Ctesias was a Greek doctor of the fifth century B.C.E. who wrote books on Persia and India.

striking varieties in the shape and habits of the body. All these facts, for which it is easy to furnish incontestable proofs, can surprise only those who are accustomed to looking solely at the objects around them, and are ignorant of the powerful effects of differences in climates, air, foods, ways of life, habits in general, and, above all, of the astonishing force of the same causes acting continuously on long successions of generations. Today, when commerce, travels, and conquests bring different people closer together, and their ways of life grow constantly more alike as a result of frequent communication, certain national differences are found to have diminished; and, for example, everyone can see that the French of today are no longer the large, white, and blond-haired bodies described by Latin historians, although time, together with the mixture of the Franks and Normans, themselves white and blond-haired, ought to have made up for whatever the contact with the Romans may have taken away from the influence of the climate on the population's natural constitution and complexion. All these observations about the varieties that a thousand causes can produce and have in fact produced in the human species make me wonder whether various animals similar to men, taken by travelers without much examination for beasts, either because of some differences they noticed in their outward conformation or merely because these animals did not speak, might not in fact be genuine savage men whose race, dispersed in the woods in ancient times, had no occasion to develop any of its virtual faculties, had not acquired any degree of perfection, and was still in the primitive state of nature. Let me give an example of what I mean.

"In the kingdom of the Congo," says the translator of the *Histoire des voyages*, "are found many of those large animals called orangutans in the East Indies, which occupy a sort of middle ground between the human species and the baboons. Battel[71] relates that in the forests of Mayomba, in the kingdom of Loango, two kinds of monsters are found, of which the larger are called *pongos* and the others *enjocos*. [See p. 15 for a rendering of such a creature.] The former bear an exact resemblance to man, but they are much heavier and very tall. With a human face, they have very deep-set eyes. Their hands, cheeks, and ears are hairless, except for their eyebrows which are very long. Although the rest of their body is rather hairy, the hair is not very thick, and its color is brown. Finally, the only part that distinguishes them from men is their leg, which has no calf. They walk upright, holding each other by the hair of

---

[71] Andrew Battel (ca. 1565–1645) was an English traveler who spent time in West Africa around 1590 and told of his adventures to Samuel Purchas (1577–1626), who recorded them.

the neck; they live in the woods; they sleep in trees, and there they build a kind of roof, which shelters them from rain. Their food is fruit or wild nuts. They never eat flesh. The custom of negroes who cross the forests is to light fires during the night; they notice that in the morning, at their departure, the pongos take their place around the fire, and do not leave until it is out; for with all their cleverness, they do not have enough sense to keep it going by bringing wood to it.

"They sometimes walk in groups and kill the negroes who traverse the forests. They even fall upon elephants that come to graze in the places they inhabit, and annoy them so with punches or sticks that they force them to flee roaring. Pongos are never taken alive because they are so robust that ten men would not be enough to stop them. But the negroes take many of their young after killing the mother, to whose body the young cling tightly. When one of these animals dies, the others cover its body with a heap of branches or leaves. Purchas adds that in the conversations he had with Battel he learned from him that a pongo kidnapped a little negro who spent a whole month in the society of these animals, for they do no harm to the human beings they take by surprise, at least not when these do not pay attention to them, as the little negro had observed. Battel did not describe the second species of monster.

"Dapper[72] confirms that the kingdom of the Congo is full of those animals which in the Indies have the name orangutans, that is to say, inhabitants of the woods, and which the Africans call *quojas morros*. This beast, he says, is so similar to man that it occurred to some travelers that it might have issued from a woman and a monkey: a myth which even the negroes reject. One of these animals was transported from the Congo to Holland, and presented to the Prince of Orange, Frederick-Henry. It was the height of a three-year-old child, and moderately stocky but square and well-proportioned, very agile and lively, its legs fleshy and robust, the whole front of its body naked but the back covered with black hair. At first sight its face resembled that of a man, but it had a flat and upturned nose; its ears were also those of the human species; its breast, for it was a female, was plump, its navel sunken, its shoulders very well joined, its hands divided into fingers and thumbs, its calves and heels fat and fleshy. It often walked upright on its legs; it was able to lift and carry rather heavy loads. When it wanted to drink, it took the cover of the pot in one hand, and held the bottom with the other, afterward it graciously wiped its lips. It lay down to sleep with its head

---

[72] Olfert Dapper (ca. 1635–1689) was a Dutch physician and geographer.

on a pillow, covering itself so skillfully that one would have taken it for a man in bed. The negroes tell strange stories about this animal. They maintain not only that it does violence to women and girls, but that it dares to attack armed men. In a word, there is great likelihood that it is the satyr of the ancients. Perhaps Merolla[73] is only referring to these animals when he relates that negroes sometimes capture savage men and women in their hunts."

These species of anthropomorphic animals are spoken of again in the third volume of the same *Histoire des voyages* under the name of *beggos* and *mandrills*. But sticking to the preceding reports, one finds in the description of these supposed monsters striking conformities with the human species, and smaller differences than those which could be assigned between one man and another. It is not clear from these passages what the authors' reasons are for refusing to call the animals in question savage men; but it is easy to conjecture that it is due to their stupidity and also because they did not speak; weak reasons for those who know that, although the organ of speech is natural to man, speech itself is nonetheless not natural to him, and who know to what point his perfectibility may have raised civil man above his original state. The small number of lines comprising these descriptions permits us to judge how poorly these animals have been observed, and with what prejudices they were seen. For example, they are characterized as monsters, and yet it is agreed that they reproduce. In one place, Battel says that pongos kill negroes who cross the forests; in another, Purchas adds that they do not do them any harm, even when they surprise them, at least not when the negroes do not insist on looking at them. The pongos gather around the fires lit by the negroes once these have left, and they in turn leave when the fire is out; there is the fact. Here, now, is the observer's commentary: *for with all their cleverness, they do not have enough sense to keep it going by bringing wood to it.* I would like to guess how Battel, or Purchas, his compiler, could have known that the pongos' departure was an effect of their stupidity rather than their will. In a climate such as Loango, fire is not a very necessary thing for animals; and if the negroes light it, it is less against the cold than to frighten wild beasts. It is therefore very simply that having enjoyed the blaze for some time, or being well warmed, the pongos get bored with always staying in the same place and go off to find food, which requires more time than if they ate

---

[73] Jerome Merolla (ca. 1650–ca. 1710) spent ten years as a Franciscan missionary in the Congo and wrote an account of it, which appeared in 1692.

flesh. Besides, it is known that most animals, not excepting man, are naturally lazy and they deny themselves all kinds of cares that are not of an absolute necessity. Finally, it seems very strange that the pongos whose skill and strength are praised, the pongos who know how to bury their dead and make themselves roofs out of branches, should not know how to push wood into the fire. I remember having seen a monkey perform the same maneuver that it is claimed a pongo cannot do. It is true that, since my ideas were not at the time being turned in that direction, I myself committed the error for which I reproach our travelers, and I neglected to examine whether the monkey's intention was in fact to sustain the fire or simply, as I believe, to imitate the action of a human being. Whatever the case, it is well demonstrated that the monkey is not a variety of man, not only because he is deprived of the faculty of speech, but above all because it is certain that his species lacks the faculty of perfecting itself, which is the specific characteristic of the human species. Experiments which seem not to have been conducted sufficiently carefully on the pongo and the orangutan allow for the same conclusion to be drawn. There would, however, be a means by which, if the orangutan or others were of the human species, the crudest observers could assure themselves of it even by demonstration. But besides the fact that a single generation would not suffice for this experiment, it must pass as impracticable, because it would be necessary that what is only a supposition were shown to be true before the test that ought to verify the fact could be tried innocently.

Precipitous judgments that are not the fruit of enlightened reason are prone to be excessive. Our travelers do not hesitate to take for beasts, under the names *pongos, mandrills, orangutans*, the same beings that the ancients, under the names *satyrs, fauns, sylvans*, made into divinities. Perhaps, after more precise research, it will be found that they are **neither animals nor gods, but** men. In the meantime, it seems to me that there is as much reason to defer on this to Merolla, an educated monk, an eyewitness, and one who, with all his naïveté, was nonetheless a man of wit, as to the merchant Battel, Dapper, Purchas, and the other compilers.

What would have been the judgment of such observers about the child found in 1694, of whom I spoke above, who gave no sign of reason, walked on his hands and feet, had no language, and formed sounds having no resemblance whatever to those of a man? It took him a long time, continues the same philosopher who provided me with this fact, before he could utter a few words, and then he did it in a barbarous way. As soon as he could speak, he was questioned about his first state, but he no more remembered it than we remember what happened to us in the cradle. If, unfortunately for him, this child had fallen into our travelers' hands, there can be no doubt that after taking note of his silence and stupidity, they would have decided to send him back to the woods or lock him up in a zoo; after which they would have spoken learnedly of him in fine reports as a very curious beast which looked rather like man.

For the three or four hundred years since the inhabitants of Europe have inundated the other parts of the world, and continually published new collections of voyages and reports, I am convinced that we know no other men except the Europeans; furthermore, it appears, from the ridiculous prejudices that have not been extinguished even among men of letters, that under the pompous name of the study of man everyone does hardly anything except study the men of his country. In vain do individuals come and go; it seems that philosophy does not travel. In addition, the philosophy of each people is but little suited for another. The cause of this is manifest, at least for distant countries; there are scarcely more than four sorts of men who make voyages of long duration: sailors, merchants, soldiers, and missionaries. Now it can hardly be expected that the first three classes should provide good observers; and as for those in the fourth, occupied by the sublime vocation that calls them, even if they were not subject to the same prejudices of status as are all the others, one has to believe that they would not voluntarily apply themselves to research that appears to be pure curiosity, and which would distract them from the more important works to which they are destined. Besides, to preach the Gospel usefully, zeal alone is necessary and God gives the rest; but to study men, talents are necessary that God is not obligated to give anyone, and that are not always the lot of saints. One cannot open a book of voyages without finding descriptions of characters and *mœurs*. But one is completely amazed to see that these people who have described so many things have said only what everyone already knew, that all they were able to see at the other end of the world is what they could perfectly well have noticed without leaving their street; and that those true features that differentiate nations and strike eyes made to see have almost always escaped theirs. Hence that fine moral adage, so often repeated by the philosophizing rabble: That men are everywhere the same; that, since they have the same passions and the same vices everywhere, it is rather useless to seek to characterize different peoples—which is about as well argued as if one were to say that it is impossible to distinguish Peter from James, because they both have a nose, a mouth, and eyes.

Will we never see reborn the happy times when people did not dabble in philosophy, but when a Plato, a Thales,[74] a Pythagoras,[75] seized with an ardent desire to know, undertook the greatest voyages merely in order to inform themselves, and went far away to shake off the yoke of national prejudices, to learn to know men by their likenesses and their differences, and to acquire that universal knowledge that is not that of one century or one country exclusively, but which, being of all times and all places, is so to speak the common science of the wise?

One admires the magnificence of some curious people who have, at great expense, made or arranged voyages to the Orient with learned men and painters, in order to draw pictures of ruins there and to decipher or copy inscriptions. But I have trouble understanding how, in a century that prides itself on great knowledge, there are not to be found two like-minded men—rich, one in money and the other in genius, both loving glory and aspiring to immortality—one of whom would sacrifice twenty thousand crowns of his wealth and the other ten years of his life for the sake of a famous voyage around the world, in order to study, not forever stones and plants, but, for once men and *mœurs*, and who, after so many centuries spent in measuring and examining the house, should finally make up their minds to want to know its inhabitants.

The academicians who have traveled through the northern parts of Europe and the southern parts of America had as object to visit them as geometers rather than as philosophers. However, since they were both at once, the regions seen and described by men such as La Condamine[76] and Maupertuis[77] cannot be regarded as entirely unknown. The jeweler Chardin,[78] who traveled like Plato, has left nothing more to be said about Persia. China seems to have been well observed by the Jesuits. Kaempfer[79] gives a tolerable idea of the little he saw in Japan. Except for these reports, we know nothing of the peoples of the East Indies, who have exclusively been visited by Europeans more interested in filling their purses than their heads. All of Africa and its numerous inhabitants, as distinctive in character as in color, are still to be exam-

---

[74] Many people regard Thales (ca. 624–ca. 546 B.C.E.) as the first Greek philosopher.

[75] Pythagoras (ca. 570–495 B.C.E.) was a Greek philosopher and religious teacher.

[76] A French explorer, Charles Marie de La Condamine (1701–1774) traveled to the Amazon and published a journal about his voyage in 1751.

[77] French mathematician Pierre Louis Moreau de Maupertuis (1698–1759) made an expedition to Lapland to conduct research and published his findings.

[78] Jean Chardin (1643–1713) traveled through Persia to India and Japan and published an account of it in *The Travels of Sir John Chardin*.

[79] Engelbert Kaempfer (1651–1716) was a German naturalist and physician who traveled to the Far East and published an account of his trip.

ined; the whole earth is covered by nations of which we know only the names—and yet we dabble in judging humankind! Let us suppose a Montesquieu, Buffon, Diderot, Duclos, d'Alembert, Condillac,[80] or men of that stamp traveling in order to instruct their compatriots, observing and describing, as they know how, Turkey, Egypt, Barbary, the empire of Morocco, Guinea, the land of the Bantus, the interior of Africa and its eastern coasts, the Malabars, Mogul, the banks of the Ganges, the kingdoms of Siam, Pegu, and Ava, China, Tartary, and especially Japan; then, in the other hemisphere, Mexico, Peru, Chile, the straits of Magellan, not forgetting the Patagonias true or false, Tucuman, Paraguay if possible, Brazil; finally the Caribbean islands, Florida, and all the savage countries: the most important voyage of all and the one that must be undertaken with the greatest care. Let us suppose that these new Hercules, back from these memorable expeditions, then at leisure wrote the natural, moral, and political history of what they had seen; then we ourselves would see a new world issue from their pen, and we would thus learn to know our own. I say that when such observers will assert about a given animal that it is a man and about another that it is a beast, they will have to be believed; but it would be too simpleminded to defer to coarse travelers about whom one might sometimes be tempted to ask the same question they pretend to answer about other animals.

XI) That seems most evident to me, and I cannot conceive from where our philosophers derive all the passions they ascribe to natural man. With the sole exception of the physically necessary, which nature itself requires, all our other needs are such only by habit, prior to which they were not needs, or by our desires, and one does not desire what one is not capable of knowing. From which it follows that savage man, desiring only the things he knows and knowing only those things the possession of which is in his power or easy to acquire, nothing should be so tranquil as his soul and nothing so limited as his mind.

XII) I find in Locke's *On Civil Government*[81] an objection which seems to me too specious for me to be allowed to ignore it. "The purpose of the association between male and female," says the philosopher, "being not simply to procreate, but to continue the species, this association ought to last, even after procreation, as long as is necessary for the nourishment and support of the young ones, that is to say, until they are capable

[80] These men were all prominent members of the French Enlightenment.
[81] Rousseau is referring to Locke's *Second Treatise of Government*, chap. 7, "Of Civil or Political Society," para. 79 and 80.

of seeing to their needs themselves. This rule, which the infinite wisdom of the Creator hath established upon the works of his hands, we see the creatures inferior to man observing constantly and exactly. In those animals which live on grass, the association between male and female lasts no longer than each act of copulation, because the teats of the mother being sufficient to nourish the young until they are capable of feeding on grass, the male is content to beget and no longer mingles with the female or the young, to whose subsistence he can contribute nothing. But in beasts of prey the association lasts longer, because the mother not being able to see to her own sustenance and at the same time feed her young by her own prey alone, a more laborious as well as more dangerous way of feeding than by feeding on grass, the assistance of the male is quite necessary to the maintenance of their common family, if one may use that term, which cannot subsist but by the joint care of the male and female until they can go find prey for themselves. The same is to be noted in all birds (except for some domestic ones which are found in places where the continual abundance of food exempts the male from the effort of feeding the young). One observes that while the young in their nest need food, the male and female bring it to them until these little ones can fly and see to their own sustenance.

"And herein, I think, lies the principal if not the only, reason why the male and female in humankind are obliged to live in a longer association than other creatures, viz., because the female is capable of conceiving, and is commonly pregnant again and makes a new child, long before the previous one is beyond needing the help of his parents, can see to his needs himself; whereby the father, who is obliged to take care of those he has begot, and to take that care for a long time, he is also under obligation to continue to live in conjugal society with the same woman by whom he had them, and to remain in that society much longer than other creatures, whose young being able to subsist by themselves before the time of a new procreation returns again, until the bond of the male and female dissolves by itself, and both find themselves at complete liberty, until such time as that season, which usually solicits the animals to join together, obliges them to choose new mates. And here one cannot but admire the wisdom of the Creator who, having given to man the qualities needed to provide for the future as well as the present, wanted and brought it about that the society of man should last much longer than that of the male and female of other creatures, so that thereby the industry of man and woman might be stimulated more, and that their interests might be better united, with a view to making provisions for their children and to leaving them goods—nothing being more to the detriment of children than an uncertain and vague association, or an easy and frequent dissolution of the conjugal society."

The same love of truth which made me sincerely set forth this objection, prompts me to accompany it with a few remarks, if not to resolve it, at least to clarify it.

1. I will observe first that moral proofs do not have great force in matters of physics, and that they serve rather to explain existing facts than to ascertain the real existence of those facts. Now such is the kind of proof Mr. Locke uses in the passage I have just quoted; for although it may be advantageous to the human species for the union between man and woman to be permanent, it does not follow that it was thus established by nature; otherwise it would be necessary to say that nature also instituted civil society, the arts, commerce, and all that is claimed to be useful to men.

2. I do not know where Mr. Locke found out that among animals of prey the association of male and female lasts longer than among those that live on grass, and that the former helps the latter to feed the young: For it is not observed that the dog, cat, bear, or wolf recognize their female better than the horse, ram, bull stag, or all the other quadrupeds recognize theirs. It seems on the contrary that if the help of the male were necessary to the female to preserve her young, it would be above all in the species that live only on grass, because the mother needs a very long time to graze, and during the entire period she is forced to neglect her brood; whereas the prey of a female bear or wolf is devoured in an instant, and she has more time, without suffering from hunger, to nurse her young. This line of reasoning is confirmed by an observation upon the relative number of teats and young which distinguishes the carnivorous species from the frugivorous, and about which I spoke in note (VIII). If this observation is correct and general, as woman has only two teats and rarely produces more than one child at a time, there is one more strong reason to doubt that the human species is naturally carnivorous. So it seems that in order to draw Locke's conclusion, his reasoning would have to be altogether reversed. There is no more solidity in the same distinction applied to birds. For who can be persuaded that the union of male and female is more durable among vultures and ravens than among turtledoves? We have two species of domestic birds, the duck and the pigeon, which provide us with examples directly contrary to the system of this author. The pigeon, which lives solely on grain, remains united with its female, and they feed their young in common. The duck, whose voraciousness is known, recognizes neither its

female nor its young, and does nothing to help with their subsistence; and among hens, a species hardly less carnivorous, it is not observed that the rooster troubles himself in the least for the brood. And if in other species the male shares with the female the care of feeding the young, it is because birds, which at first cannot fly and which the mother cannot nurse, are much less able to do without the assistance of the father than are quadrupeds, for which the mother's teat suffices, at least for some time.

3. There is much uncertainty about the principal fact that serves as a basis for all of Mr. Locke's reasoning: For in order to know whether, as he claims, in the pure state of nature the woman is ordinarily pregnant again and has another child long before the preceding one can himself provide for his needs, it would be necessary to make experiments that Mr. Locke surely did not make and that no one is able to make. The continual cohabitation of husband and wife provides such an immediate opportunity to be exposed to a new pregnancy that it is very hard to believe that chance encounter or the impulsion of temperament alone produced such frequent effects in the pure state of nature as in the state of conjugal society—a slowness that would perhaps tend to make the children more robust, and that in addition might be compensated by a prolonged ability to conceive among women, who would have abused it less in their youth. With regard to children, there are many reasons to believe that their strength and their organs develop later among us than they did in the primitive state of which I speak. The original weakness they derive from the constitution of their parents, the cares taken to wrap and restrain all their limbs, the softness in which they are raised, perhaps the use of milk other than their mother's, everything thwarts and retards in them the first progress of nature. The concentration they are obliged to give to a thousand things on which their attention is continually fixed, while no exercise is given to their bodily strength, may also bring about considerable diversion in their growth; so that if instead of first overburdening and tiring their minds in a thousand ways, their bodies were left to be exercised by the continual movements that nature seems to demand of them, it is to be presumed that they would much sooner be capable of walking, acting, and providing for their needs themselves.

4. Finally, Mr. Locke proves at most that there could well be in a man a motive for remaining attached to a woman when she has a child; but he does not prove at all that he must have been attached to her before the delivery and during the nine months of pregnancy. If a given woman is indifferent to the man during these nine months, if she even

becomes unknown to him, why will he assist her after delivery? Why will he help her to raise a child he does not even know belongs to him, and whose birth he neither planned nor foresaw? Mr. Locke evidently supposes what is in question; for it is not a matter of knowing why the man will remain attached to the woman after delivery, but why he will become attached to her after conception. Once his appetite is satisfied, the man no longer needs a given woman, nor the woman a given man. The man has not the least concern nor perhaps the least idea of the consequences of his action. One goes off in one direction, the other in another, and there is no likelihood that at the end of nine months they have any memory of having known each other: For this kind of memory, by which one individual gives preference to another for the act of procreation, requires, as I prove in the text, more progress or corruption in human understanding than can be supposed in man in the state of animality in question here. Another woman can therefore satisfy the new desires of the man as conveniently as the one he has already known, and another man satisfy in the same way the woman, supposing that she is impelled by the same appetite during pregnancy, which can reasonably be doubted. And if in the state of nature the woman no longer feels the passion of love after the conception of the child, the obstacle to her society with the man thereby becomes much greater still, since then she no longer needs either the man who impregnated her or any other. Therefore there is not, for the man, any reason to seek the same woman, nor for the woman, any reason to seek the same man. Locke's reasoning therefore falls apart, and all the dialectic of this philosopher has not saved him from the error committed by Hobbes and others. They had to explain a fact of the state of nature, that is to say, of a state where men lived isolated and where a given man had no motive for living near another given man, nor perhaps to live near one another, which is much worse; and they did not think of carrying themselves back beyond the centuries of society, that is to say, of those times when men have always had a reason to live near one another, and when a given man often has a reason for living beside a given man or a given woman.

XIII) I will refrain from launching into the philosophic reflections to be made about the advantages and inconveniences of this institution of languages; it is not for me to be permitted to attack vulgar errors, and educated people respect their prejudices too much to bear my supposed paradoxes patiently. Let us therefore let speak the men in whom it is not deemed a crime to dare sometimes to take the side of reason against the opinion of the multitude. "Nor would any of the happiness of the human race disappear if, when the crowd and confusion of so many languages has been expelled, [all] mortals should cultivate [this] one art and if it should be permitted to explain everything with signs, movements, and actions. But now it has so been established that the condition of animals that are popularly believed to be brutes is far better than ours in this regard, inasmuch as they indicate their feelings and thoughts without an interpreter more readily and perhaps more happily than any mortals can, especially when they are using a foreign language." (Isaac Vossius, *De Poematum Cantu et Viribus Rythmi* (Oxford: Theatro Sheldoniano, 1673), pp. 65–66.)

XIV) Plato, showing how necessary ideas of discrete quantity and its relations are in the lesser arts, rightly mocks the authors of his time who claimed that Palamedes[82] had invented numbers at the siege of Troy; as if, says this philosopher, Agamemnon could have been ignorant until then of how many legs he had. Indeed, one senses how impossible it is for society and the arts to have reached the level they already were at by the time of the siege of Troy, without men's having the use of numbers and arithmetic. But the need to know numbers, before acquiring other knowledge, does not make their invention easier to imagine. Once the names of the numbers are known, it is easy to explain their meaning and elicit the ideas these names represent; but in order to invent them it was necessary, before conceiving of these same ideas, to be, so to speak, familiar with philosophic meditations, to be trained in considering beings by their sole essence and independently of all other perception: A very difficult, very metaphysical, not very natural abstraction, and one without which, nevertheless, these ideas could never have been carried from one species or genus to another, nor could numbers have become universal. A savage could consider separately his right leg and his left leg, or view them together in terms of the indivisible idea of a pair, without ever thinking that he had two of them; for the representative idea that depicts an object to us is one thing, and the numerical idea that determines it is another. Even less could he count to five; and although by placing his hands on one another, he could have noticed that the fingers matched exactly, he was very far from thinking of their numerical equality. He did not know the sum of his fingers any more than that of his hairs; and if, after having made him understand what numbers are, someone said to him that he had as many toes as fingers,

---

[82] Palamedes was a character out of Greek mythology who was given credit for several inventions, such as numbers, the alphabet, and currency.

he would perhaps have been very surprised, in comparing them to find it was true.

XV) One should not confuse *Amour propre* and *Amour de soi-même*, two passions very different in their nature and their effects.[83] *Amour de soi-même* is a natural sentiment which inclines every animal to take care of its own preservation, and which, directed in man by reason and modified by pity, produces humanity and virtue. *Amour propre* is only a relative sentiment, artificial and born in society, which inclines each individual to have a greater esteem for himself than for anyone else, which inspires in men all the harm they do to one another, and which is the true source of honor.

This being well understood, I say that in our primitive state, in the true state of nature, *Amour propre* does not exist. For since each individual man regards himself as the only spectator to observe him, as the only being in the universe to take an interest in him, and as the only judge of his own merit, it is not possible that a sentiment which originates in comparisons he is not capable of making could spring up in his soul. For the same reason this man could have neither hate nor desire for revenge, passions that can arise only from the opinion that some offense has been received; and as it is scorn or intention to hurt and not the harm that constitutes the offense, men who know neither how to evaluate themselves nor compare themselves can do each other a great deal of mutual violence when they derive some advantage from it, without ever offending one another. In a word, every man, seeing his fellow men hardly otherwise than he would see animals of another species, can carry off the prey of the weaker or relinquish his own to the stronger, without considering these plunderings as anything but natural events, without the slightest emotion of insolence or spite, and with no other passion than the sadness or joy of a good or bad outcome.

XVI) It is an extremely remarkable thing, for all the years the Europeans have been tormenting themselves to bring the savages of various countries in the world over to their way of life, that they have not yet been able to win over a single one of them, not even with the aid of Christianity; for our missionaries sometimes make Christians of them, but never civilized men. Nothing can overcome the invincible repugnance they have against adopting our *mœurs* and living in our way. If these poor

---

[83] Rousseau here describes a distinction that is fundamental to his moral psychology. He would use it, and build upon it, in his later writings.

savages are as unhappy as it is claimed they are, by what inconceivable depravity of judgment do they constantly refuse to civilize themselves by imitating us or to learn to live happily among us; whereas one reads in a thousand places that Frenchmen and other Europeans have voluntarily taken refuge among these nations, spent their entire lives there, without any longer being able to leave such a strange way of life and one even sees sensible missionaries regret with emotion the calm and innocent days they spent among such greatly scorned peoples? If one answers that they do not have enough enlightenment to judge soundly about their state and ours, I will reply that the estimation of happiness is less the affair of reason than of sentiment. Besides, this reply can be turned against us with even more force; for there is a greater distance between our ideas and the mental disposition necessary in order to conceive of the taste that savages find for their way of life than between the ideas of savages and those that can allow them to conceive of our way of life. Indeed, after several observations it is easy for them to see that all our labors are directed toward only two objects; namely, the commodities of life for oneself, and consideration among others. But how are we to imagine the kind of pleasure a savage takes in spending his life alone in the middle of the woods, or fishing, or blowing into a bad flute, without ever knowing how to get a single tone from it and without troubling himself to learn?

Savages have several times been brought to Paris, London, and other cities; people have hurried to show off our luxury, our wealth, and all our most useful and curious arts; all this has never aroused in them anything except stupid admiration, without the slightest stirring of covetousness. I recall among others the story of a chief of some North Americans who was brought to the court of England some thirty years ago. A thousand things were put before his eyes to try to give him some present that could please him, but nothing could be found about which he seemed to care. Our weapons seemed heavy and inconvenient to him; our shoes hurt his feet, our clothes confined him, he refused everything; finally someone observed that having taken a woolen blanket, he seemed to take pleasure in wrapping it around his shoulders. You will at least agree, someone promptly said to him, about the usefulness of this furnishing? Yes, he replied, it seems to me almost as good as an animal skin. And he would not even have said that if he had worn them both in the rain.

Perhaps, someone will say to me, it is habit, which, by attaching everyone to his way of life, prevents savages from sensing what is good in ours. And on that basis it must at least appear very extraordinary that habit has more strength in maintaining the savages' taste for their misery than in maintaining Europeans in the enjoyment of their felicity. But to reply to this last objection with an answer to which there is not a word of rejoinder—without citing all the young savages whom people have tried in vain to civilize, without speaking of the Greenlanders and inhabitants of Iceland, whom people tried to raise and feed in Denmark and all of whom sadness and despair caused to perish, either from languor or in the sea when they tried to swim back to their homeland—I shall be content to cite a single, well-authenticated example, which I offer for the examination of admirers of European civilization.

"All the efforts of the Dutch missionaries at the Cape of Good Hope have never been able to convert a single Hottentot. Van der Stel, governor of the Cape, having taken one from infancy, had him raised in the principles of the Christian religion and in the practice of European customs. He was richly dressed, he was taught several languages, and his progress corresponded very well to the cares taken for his education. The governor, placing great hopes in his intelligence, sent him to the Indies with a general commissioner who employed him usefully in the affairs of the company. He returned to the Cape after the death of the commissioner. A few days after his return, during a visit he paid to some of his Hottentot relatives he made the decision to divest himself of his European finery in order to clothe himself in a sheepskin. He returned to the fort in this new garb, carrying a package which contained his old clothes, and presenting them to the governor, he made this speech: *Be so kind, sir, as to understand that I renounce this paraphernalia forever; I renounce also for my entire life the Christian religion; my resolution is to live and die in the religion, ways, and customs of my ancestors. The sole favor I ask of you is to let me keep the necklace and cutlass I am wearing; I will keep them for love of you.* Immediately, without awaiting Van der Stel's reply, he escaped by running away and he was never seen again at the Cape." *Histoire des voyages*, volume 5, page 175.

(Opposite) **Figure 3.** This image illustrates the story Rousseau tells in Note XVI about a native who leaves European civilization in order to "return to his equals." It was originally used as the frontispiece of the Second Discourse.

Frontispiece of a German edition of *Discourse on Inequality*, by Jean-Jacques Rousseau (1712–1778), published by Christian Friedrich Voss, Berlin, 1756 (engraving) by German School (18th century) Deutsches Historisches Museum, Berlin, Germany / © DHM / The Bridgeman Art Library.

XVII) One could object that, in such a disorder, men, instead of stubbornly murdering one another, would have dispersed if there had been no limits on their dispersion. But first, these limits would at least have been those of the world; and if one thinks of the excessive population which results from the state of nature, one will judge that it would not have been long before the earth, in that state, was covered with men, thus forced to remain together. Besides, they would have dispersed if the evil had been rapid, and had it been a change occurring overnight. But they were born under the yoke; they were in the habit of bearing it when they felt its weight, and they were content to wait for the opportunity to shake it off. Finally, as they were already accustomed to a thousand comforts which forced them to remain together, dispersion was no longer so easy as in the first ages, when no one having need of anyone but himself, everyone made his decision without waiting for the consent of another.

XVIII) Marshal de V*** related that, in one of his campaigns, the excessive knavery of a food agent having made the army suffer and complain, he berated him severely and threatened to have him hanged. This threat does not bother me, the knave boldly answered him, and I am very happy to tell you that a man who has a hundred thousand crowns at his disposal does not get hanged. I do not know how it happened, the Marshal added naïvely, but in fact he was not hanged, although he had deserved it a hundred times.

XIX) Distributive justice would still be opposed to this rigorous equality of the state of nature, even if it were practicable in civil society; and as all the members of the state owe it services proportionate to their talents and strengths, the citizens in their turn ought to be distinguished and favored in proportion to their services. It is in this sense that a passage of Isocrates[84] must be understood, in which he praises the first Athenians for having well known how to distinguish which was the most advantageous of the two sorts of equality, one of which consists in dividing the same advantages among all citizens indifferently, and the other in distributing them according to each one's merit. These skillful politicians, adds the orator, banishing that unjust equality which establishes no difference between evil and good men, adhered inviolably to that which rewards and punishes everyone according to his merit. But first, no society has ever existed, whatever degree of corruption

[84] Isocrates (436–338 B.C.E.) was a famous ancient Greek orator and rhetorician.

societies might have reached, in which no difference between evil and good men was established; and in matters of *mœurs*—where the law cannot establish an exact enough measurement to serve as a rule for the magistrate—the law very wisely, in order not to leave the fate or rank of citizens at his discretion, forbids him the judgment of persons, leaving him only that of actions. Only *mœurs* as pure as those of the ancient Romans can bear censors; such tribunals would soon have overthrown everything among us. It is up to public esteem to establish the difference between evil and good men. The magistrate is judge only of rigorous right; but the people are the true judges of *mœurs*: an upright and even enlightened judge on this point, sometimes deceived but never corrupted. The ranks of citizens therefore ought to be regulated not upon their personal merit, which would be leaving to the magistrates the means of making an almost arbitrary application of the law, but upon the real services that they render to the state, which are susceptible of a more exact assessment.

PART THREE

Related Documents

1

JACQUES-BÉNIGNE BOSSUET

Politics Drawn from the Very Words of Holy Scripture

1709

Jacques-Bénigne Bossuet (1627–1704) was born in Dijon, France, to a family of lawyers and judges. Educated for a career in the church, he was ordained a priest and received his doctorate in theology in 1652. He proved himself to be a brilliant controversialist and an eloquent preacher, which brought him to the attention of Louis XIV. He became a bishop in 1670 and was appointed tutor to the king's son. For a short while he also served as the king's spiritual adviser. It was during his time at court that Bossuet wrote the first six books of his Politics, *which he completed years later and which was published posthumously in 1709. It is recognized as the most authoritative defense of the divine right of kings in French political thought.*

From Jacques-Bénigne Bossuet, *Politics Drawn from the Very Words of Holy Scripture*, ed and trans. Patrick Riley (Cambridge, U.K.: Cambridge University Press, 1999), 3–4, 8–10, 14–18, 57–60, 81.

First Book: Of the principles of human society

FIRST ARTICLE. MAN IS MADE TO LIVE IN SOCIETY

1st Proposition: Men have but one and the same end and one and the same object, which is God . . .

2nd Proposition: The love of God obliges men to love one another . . .

3rd Proposition: All men are brothers . . .

ARTICLE II. THE SOCIETY OF MANKIND GIVES BIRTH TO CIVIL SOCIETY, THAT IS TO SAY, TO STATES, PEOPLES, AND NATIONS

1st Proposition: Human society has been destroyed and violated by the passions

God was the bond of human society. The first man having separated himself from God, by a just punishment division was cast in his family, and Cain killed his brother Abel.[1]

The whole of the human race was divided. The children of Seth were called the children of God; and the children of Cain were called the children of men.[2]

These two races, by their alliances, only augmented corruption. . . .

"All the thoughts of men turned at all times to evil, and God repented of having made them. Noah alone found grace before him," so general was the corruption.[3]

It is easy to comprehend that this perversity renders men unsociable. Man governed by his passions, thinks only of satisfying them without considering others. . . .

All the passions are insatiable. . . .

Jealousy, so universal among men, exposes the profound malignity of their hearts. Our brother does us no injury, he takes nothing from us; nevertheless, he becomes to us an object of hatred, only because we see him more happy, or more industrious, or more virtuous than ourselves. . . .

From so many insensate passions, and so many different interests arising from them, results that there is no faith to be reposed, or safety to be found among men. . . . There is nothing so brutal or so sangui-

---

[1] Genesis 4:8.
[2] Genesis 6:2. Seth was the child born to Adam and Eve after Abel's death.
[3] Genesis 6:5, 6, 8, 11.

nary as man. "All lie in wait for blood; every one hunteth his brother to death."[4]

"Cursing, and lying, and killing, and theft, and adultery have overflowed, and blood hath touched blood,"[5] that is to say, that one murder draws on another.

Thus human society, established by so many sacred bonds, is violated by the passions, and as St. Augustine[6] says: "There is nothing more sociable than man by nature, or more unsociable than man by corruption."[7] ...

ARTICLE III. TO FORM NATIONS AND UNITE THE PEOPLE, IT IS NECESSARY TO HAVE A GOVERNMENT ...

2nd Proposition: Only the authority of government puts a bridle on the passions, and to the violence become natural to men ...

3rd Proposition: It is by the sole authority of government that union is established among men ...

4th Proposition: In a regulated government, each individual renounces the right of occupying by force what he finds suitable

Take away the government, the earth and all its goods are as common among men, as the air and the light. God said to all men: "Increase and multiply, and fill the earth."[8] He gave to them all, indiscriminately, "every herb bearing seed upon the earth, and all trees that have in themselves seed of their own kind."[9] According to this right of nature, no one has a particular right to any thing whatever, and everything is the prey of all. ...

Moses ordained, after the conquest of the land of Canaan, that it should be distributed to the people by the authority of the sovereign magistrate. ...

From thence arose the right of property; and in general all rights should come from the public authority. ...

5th Proposition: By the government each individual becomes stronger

[4] Micah 2.
[5] Hosea 4:2.
[6] Augustine of Hippo (354–430) was an important Christian theologian.
[7] St. Augustine, *De civitate dei* I. xii, xxv.
[8] Genesis 1:28; 9:7.
[9] Genesis 1:29.

The reason is that each one is secured. All the powers of the nation center in one, and the sovereign magistrate has the right to combine them. . . .

Thus the sovereign magistrate has in his hands all the strength of the nation, which submits to, and obeys him. . . .

All strength is transferred to the sovereign magistrate: every one strengthens him to the prejudice of his own, and renounces his own life in case of disobedience. . . .

. . . There is no state worse than that of anarchy, that is to say, a state in which every one would do all that he wills; no one will do that which he wills; where there is no master, every one is master; where every one is master, every one is a slave. . . .

Third Book: In which one begins to explain the nature and the properties of royal authority . . .

ARTICLE II. ROYAL AUTHORITY IS SACRED

1st Proposition: God establishes kings as his ministers, and reigns through them over the peoples . . .

2nd Proposition: The person of kings is sacred

It appears from all this that the person of kings is sacred, and that to attempt anything against them is a sacrilege. . . .

One must protect kings as sacred things; and whoever neglects to guard them is worthy of death. . . .

3rd Proposition: One must obey the prince by reason of religion and conscience . . .

There is thus something religious in the respect one gives to the prince. The service of God and respect for kings are inseparable things, and St. Peter places these two duties together: "Fear God, Honor the King." . . .

Fourth Book: On the characteristics of royalty (continuation)

FIRST ARTICLE. ROYAL AUTHORITY IS ABSOLUTE . . .

2

THOMAS HOBBES

Leviathan

1651

Thomas Hobbes (1588–1679) was an enormously influential English philosopher. Although he made contributions to many fields—including history, science, theology, and philosophy in general—he is best known for his political thought. When the English Civil Wars (1642–1651) forced him into exile in Paris, he published the Leviathan, *in which he expressed his strong royalist principles. His title is a reference to a biblical sea monster; in Hobbes's rendering, however, it became a metaphor for the kind of strong state he favored. This selection reflects Hobbes's vision of human nature and why he thought authoritarian governments were necessary.*

Of the Natural Condition of Mankind, as concerning their Felicity, and Misery

Nature hath made men so equal, in the faculties of body, and mind; as that though there be found one man sometimes manifestly stronger in body, or of quicker mind than another; yet when all is reckoned together, the difference between man, and man, is not so considerable, as that one man can thereupon claim to himself any benefit, to which another may not pretend, as well as he. For as to the strength of body, the weakest has strength enough to kill the strongest, either by secret machination, or by confederacy with others, that are in the same danger with himself. . . .

From this equality of ability, ariseth equality of hope in the attaining of our ends. And therefore if any two men desire the same thing, which nevertheless they cannot both enjoy, they become enemies; and in the way to their end, (which is principally their own conservation, and sometimes their delectation only,) endeavor to destroy, or subdue one another. . . .

From Thomas Hobbes, *Leviathan, or the Matter, Form, and Power of a Commonwealth Ecclesiastical and Civil* (London: Printed for Andrew Crooke, 1651), 60–62, 85, 87.

So that in the nature of man, we find three principal causes of quarrel. First, competition; secondly, diffidence; thirdly, glory.

The first, maketh men invade for gain; the second, for safety; and the third, for reputation. The first use violence, to make themselves masters of other men's persons, wives, children, and cattle; the second, to defend them; the third, for trifles, as a word, a smile, a different opinion, and any other sign of undervalue, either direct in their persons, or by reflection in their kindred, their friends, their nation, their profession, or their name.

Hereby it is manifest, that during the time men live without a common power to keep them all in awe, they are in that condition which is called war; and such a war, as is of every man, against every man. . . . In such condition, there is . . . continual fear, and danger of violent death; And the life of man, solitary, poor, nasty, brutish, and short. . . .

Of the Causes, Generation, and Definition of a Common-wealth

The final cause, end, or design of men, (who naturally love liberty, and dominion over others,) . . . is . . . getting themselves out from that miserable condition of war. . . .

The only way to erect such a common power, as may be able to defend them from the invasion of foreigners, and the injuries of one another, and thereby to secure them in such sort, as that by their own industry, and by the fruits of the earth, they may nourish themselves and live contentedly; is, to confer all their power and strength upon one man, or upon one assembly of men. . . . This done, the multitude so united in one person, is called a COMMON-WEALTH, in Latin CIVITAS. This is the generation of that great LEVIATHAN, or rather (to speak more reverently) of that *Mortal God*, to which we owe under the *Immortal God*, our peace and defense.

3

SAMUEL VON PUFENDORF

On the Duty of Man and Citizen
According to Natural Law
1673

The German thinker Samuel von Pufendorf (1632–1694) was the most influential natural law philosopher of the seventeenth and eighteenth centuries. A faithful Lutheran, he was influenced by the Thirty Years' War, which devastated Germany. His major work of philosophy, Of the Law of Nature and Nations, *appeared in 1672. The next year he published a condensed version of it as* The Duty of Man and Citizen According to Natural Law. *In this selection Pufendorf explains why men are drawn to society and why the state is necessary.*

On men's natural state

. . . We may consider the natural state of man, by an imaginative effort, as the condition man would have been in if he had been left to himself alone, without any support from other men, given the condition of human nature as we now perceive it. It would have been, it seems, more miserable than that of any beast, if we reflect on the great weakness of man as he comes into this world, when he would straight away die without help from others, and on the primitive life he would lead if he had no other resources than he owes to his own strength and intelligence. One may put it more strongly: the fact that we have been able to grow out of such weakness, the fact that we now enjoy innumerable good things, the fact that we have cultivated our minds and bodies for our own and others' benefit—all this is the result of help from others. . . .

. . . If you picture to yourself a person (even an adult) left alone in this world without any of the aids and conveniences by which human ingenuity has relieved and enriched our lives, you will see a naked dumb

From Samuel Pufendorf, *On the Duty of Man and Citizen*, ed. James Tully, trans. Michael Silverthorne (Cambridge, U.K.: Cambridge University Press, 2000), 115–19, 132–33.

animal, without resources, seeking to satisfy his hunger with roots and grasses and his thirst with whatever water he can find, to shelter himself from the inclemencies of the weather in caves, at the mercy of wild beasts, fearful of every chance encounter. . . . To put the matter in a few words, in the state of nature each is protected only by his own strength; in the state by the strength of all. There no one may be sure of the fruit of his industry; here all may be. There is the reign of the passions, there there is war, fear, poverty, nastiness, solitude, barbarity, ignorance, savagery; here is the reign of reason, here there is peace, security, wealth, splendor, society, taste, knowledge, benevolence. . . .

Nature herself has willed that there should be a kind of kinship among men, by force of which it is wrong to harm another man and indeed right for everyone to work for the benefit of others. However, kinship usually has a rather weak force among those who live in natural liberty with each other. Consequently, we have to regard any man who is not our fellow-citizen, or with whom we live in a state of nature, not indeed as our enemy, but as a friend we cannot wholly rely on. The reason is that men not only can do each other very great harm, but do very often wish to do so for various reasons. Some are driven to injure others by their wickedness of character, or by lust for power and superfluous wealth. Others, though men of moderation, take up arms to preserve themselves and not to be forestalled by others. Many find themselves in conflict because they are competing for the same object, others through rivalry of talents. Hence in the natural state there is a lively and all but perpetual play of suspicion, distrust, eagerness to subvert the strength of others, and desire to get ahead of them or to augment one's own strength by their ruin. . . .

On the impulsive cause of constituting the state

. . . No animal is fiercer than man, none more savage and prone to more vices disruptive of the peace of society. For besides the desires for food and sex to which the beasts also are subject, man is driven by many vices unknown to them, such as, an insatiable craving for more than he needs, ambition (the most terrible of evils), too-lively remembrance of wrongs, and a burning desire for revenge which constantly grows in force over time; the infinite variety of his inclinations and appetites, and stubbornness in pressing his own causes. And man has such a furious pleasure in savaging his own kind that the greatest part of the evils to which the human condition is subject derives from man himself.

Therefore the true and principal cause why heads of households abandoned their natural liberty and had recourse to the constitution of states was to build protection around themselves against the evils that threaten man from man.

4

JOHN LOCKE

Two Treatises of Government
1690

John Locke (1632–1704) was an English physician and philosopher who lived through one of the most turbulent periods in English history. His experiences caused him to write the Two Treatises of Government, *from which the following excerpts are drawn. Locke's ideas had a profound impact on the evolution of Western political philosophy and, in particular, on the origins and development of modern liberalism. His arguments on liberty and the social contract influenced, among others, the Founding Fathers of the United States. In this excerpt, Locke offers his unique perspective on the relationship between property and the origins of government.*

Of Property

God, who hath given the world to men in common, hath also given them reason to make use of it to the best advantage of life, and convenience. . . . And though all the fruits it naturally produces, and beasts it feeds, belong to mankind in common, . . . there must, of necessity, be a means to appropriate them some way or other before they can be of any use, or at all beneficial to any particular men. . . .

From John Locke, *Two Treatises of Government* (London: Printed for Awnsham Churchill, 1690), 243–47, 345–46.

Though the earth, and all inferior creatures be common to all men, yet every man has a *property* in his own *person*. This nobody has any right to but himself. The *labor* of his body, and the *work* of his hands, we may say, are properly his. Whatsoever then he removes out of the state that nature hath provided, and left it in, he hath mixed his *labor* with it, and joined to it something that is his own, and thereby makes it his *property*. . . .

. . . Thus the grass my horse has bit; the turfs my servant has cut; and the ore I have dug in any place where I have a right to them in common with others, become my *property*, without the assignation or consent of anybody.

Of the Ends of Political Society and Government

If man in the state of nature be so free as has been said; If he be absolute lord of his own person and possessions, equal to the greatest, and subject to nobody, why will he part with his freedom, this empire, and subject himself to the dominion and control of any other power? To which 'tis obvious to answer, that though in the state of nature he hath such a right, yet the enjoyment of it is very uncertain, and constantly exposed to the invasion of others; for all being kings as much as he, every man his equal, and the greater part no strict observers of equity and justice; the enjoyment of the property he has in this state is very unsafe, very unsecure. This makes him willing to quit this condition, which however free, is full of fears and continual dangers: and 'tis not without reason, that he seeks out, and is willing to join in society with others who are already united, or have a mind to unite for the mutual preservation of their lives, liberties and estates, which I call by the general name, property.

5

GEORGE-LOUIS LECLERC DE BUFFON

Discourse on the Nature of Animals

1753

George-Louis Leclerc de Buffon (1707–1788) was a renowned French naturalist. Born in Dijon, he studied law at the university there only to find himself drawn to the fields of mathematics and science. In 1732 he moved to Paris, where he met Voltaire and other philosophes. Buffon's massive Natural History *(thirty-six volumes) aimed to organize everything that was then known of the natural world. Buffon's views influenced not only Rousseau but also the next generation of scientists, including Charles Darwin (1809–1882). This excerpt shows Buffon's use of comparison to emphasize the nobility of man. It also contains an interesting rumination on love and its ability to make men miserable.*

Discourse on the Nature of Animals

As it is only by comparing that we can judge that our knowledge depends even entirely on the relations that things have with those that resemble them or differ from them, and that if animals did not exist, the nature of man would be even more incomprehensible; after having considered man in himself, should we not make use of this means of comparison? . . . But since man is not a simple animal, since his nature is superior to that of animals, we should concern ourselves with proving the cause of this superiority, and to establish, by clear and solid proof, the precise degree of this inferiority of the nature of animals, so as to distinguish what belongs only to man, and what belongs to him in common with the animal. . . .

Animals have excellent senses, however not all the ones they have are as good as man's, and one must observe that the degrees of excellence of the senses in animals follow another order than in man. The sense that relates most to thought and understanding is touch: as we have proved, man has a more perfect sense of touch than animals. Smell is

From George-Louis Leclerc de Buffon, "Discourse on the Nature of Animals," in *Natural History, General and Particular* (Paris: Imprimerie Royale, 1753), 4:3, 5, 30, 80–82. Translated by Helena Rosenblatt.

the sense that relates most to instinct, to appetite; the animal has an infinitely better sense of smell than man: also man must understand more
than desire . . . and the animal must desire more than understand. . . .

Love! Why do you create the happiness of all creatures and the misery of man? It is because only the physical in this passion is good, it is
because, despite what the smitten might say, morals count for nothing
in it. What are, in fact, the morals in love? Vanity: vanity in the pleasure
of conquest, error that comes from making too much of it; vanity in
the desire to hold on to it exclusively; miserable condition that always
accompanies jealousy. . . . Animals are not subject to all these miseries,
they do not seek pleasures where there can be none, guided only by
sentiment, they do not err in their choice, their desires are always in
proportion to their power to enjoy them; they sense as much as they
enjoy, and only enjoy as much as they sense; man, on the contrary, by
wanting to invent pleasures, has done nothing but spoil Nature. . . . Let
man examine himself, analyze himself and become deeper, and he will
soon recognize the nobility of his being, he will feel the existence of
his soul, he will stop degrading himself, and he will see in a glance the
infinite distance that the Supreme being has placed between the animals
and himself.

6

JEAN-JACQUES ROUSSEAU

Of the Social Contract
1762

*Seven years after the publication of the Second Discourse, Rousseau
presented his views on what would constitute a legitimate social contract.
His radical reevaluation of the grounds of political legitimacy attracted
the attention of authorities in France and Geneva, where his book was
banned and burned and warrants for his arrest were issued. It remains
one of the most provocative endorsements of democracy ever written.
Paradoxically, it also expresses some principles that have been regarded
as potentially harmful to individual rights. In the following excerpts,
Rousseau expresses his commitment to both freedom and equality for each
member of the political community.*

Of the Social Pact

I assume men having reached the point where the obstacles that inter-
fere with their preservation in the state of nature prevail by their resistance over the forces which each individual can muster to maintain himself in that state. Then that primitive state can no longer subsist, and
humankind would perish if it did not change its way of being.

Now, since men cannot engender new forces, but only unite and direct
those that exist, they are left with no other means of self-preservation
than to form, by aggregation, a sum of forces that might prevail over
those obstacles' resistance, to set them in motion by a single impetus,
and make them act in concert.

This sum of forces can only arise from the cooperation of many: but
since each man's force and freedom are his primary instruments of self-
preservation, how can he commit them without harming himself, and
without neglecting the cares he owes himself? This difficulty, in relation
to my subject, can be stated in the following terms.

From Jean-Jacques Rousseau, *Of the Social Contract or Principles of Political Right*, in
The Social Contract and Other Later Political Writings, ed. and trans. Victor Gourevitch
(Cambridge, U.K.: Cambridge University Press, 1997), 49–53, 57, 59–61, 63.

"To find a form of association that will defend and protect the person and goods of each associate with the full common force, and by means of which each, uniting with all, nevertheless obey only himself and remain as free as before." This is the fundamental problem to which the social contract provides the solution.

The clauses of this contract are so completely determined by the nature of the act that the slightest modification would render them null and void; so that although they may never have been formally stated, they are everywhere the same, everywhere tacitly admitted and recognized; until, the social compact having been violated, everyone is thereupon restored to his original rights and resumes his natural freedom while losing the conventional freedom for which he renounced it.

These clauses, rightly understood, all come down to just one, namely the total alienation of each associate with all of his rights to the whole community. . . .

Moreover, since the alienation is made without reservation, the union is as perfect as it can be, and no associate has anything further to claim: For if individuals were left some rights, then, since there would be no common superior who might adjudicate between them and the public, each, being judge in his own case on some issue, would soon claim to be so on all, the state of nature would subsist and the association necessarily become tyrannical or empty.

Finally, each, by giving himself to all, gives himself to no one, and since there is no associate over whom one does not acquire the same rights as one grants him over oneself, one gains the equivalent of all one loses, and more force to preserve what one has.

If, then, one sets aside everything that is not of the essence of the social compact, one finds that it can be reduced to the following terms: *Each of us puts his person and his full power in common under the supreme direction of the general will; and in a body we receive each member as an indivisible part of the whole.*

At once, in place of the private person of each contracting party, this act of association produces a moral and collective body made up of as many members as the assembly has voices, and which receives by this same act its unity, its common *self,* its life and its will. The public person thus formed by the union of all the others formerly assumed the name *City* and now assumes that of *Republic* or of *body politic,* which its members call *State* when it is passive, *Sovereign* when active, *Power* when comparing it to similar bodies. As for the associates, they collectively assume the name *people* and individually call themselves *Citizens* as participants in the sovereign authority, and *Subjects* as subjected to the laws of the State. . . .

Of the Sovereign

This formula shows that the act of association involves a reciprocal engagement between the public and private individuals, and that each individual, by contracting, so to speak, with himself, finds himself engaged in a two-fold relation: namely as [a] member of the Sovereign toward private individuals, and as a member of the State toward the Sovereign. . . .

Indeed each individual may, as a man, have a particular will contrary to or different from the general will he has as a Citizen. His particular interest may speak to him quite differently from the common interest; his absolute and naturally independent existence may lead him to look upon what he owes to the common cause as a gratuitous contribution, the loss of which will harm others less than its payment burdens him and, by considering the moral person that constitutes the State as a being of reason because it is not a man, he would enjoy the rights of a citizen without being willing to fulfill the duties of a subject; an injustice, the progress of which would cause the ruin of the body politic.

Hence for the social compact not to be an empty formula, it tacitly includes the following engagement which alone can give force to the rest, that whoever refuses to obey the general will shall be constrained to do so by the entire body: which means nothing other than that he shall be forced to be free; for this is the condition which, by giving each Citizen to the Fatherland, guarantees him against all personal dependence; the condition which is the device and makes for the operation of the political machine, and alone renders legitimate civil engagements which would otherwise be absurd, tyrannical and liable to the most enormous abuses.

Of the Civil State

This transition from the state of nature to the civil state produces a most remarkable change in man by substituting justice for instinct in his conduct, and endowing his actions with the morality they previously lacked. Only then, when the voice of duty succeeds physical impulsion and right succeeds appetite, does man, who until then had looked only to himself, see himself forced to act on other principles, and to consult his reason before listening to his inclinations. Although in this state he deprives himself of several advantages he has from nature, he gains such great advantages in return, his faculties are exercised and developed, his ideas enlarged, his sentiments ennobled, his entire soul is elevated to such an extent, that if the abuses of this new condition did not often degrade him to beneath the condition he has left, he should ceaselessly bless the happy moment which wrested him from it forever, and out of a stupid and bounded animal made an intelligent being and a man. . . .

That Sovereignty Is Inalienable

The first and most important consequence of the principles established so far is that the general will alone can direct the forces of the State according to the end of its institution, which is the common good. . . .

I say, then, that sovereignty, since it is nothing but the exercise of the general will, can never be alienated, and that the sovereign, which is nothing but a collective being, can only be represented by itself; power can well be transferred, but not will. . . .

Whether the General Will Can Err

From the preceding it follows that the general will is always upright and always tends to the public utility: but it does not follow from it that the people's deliberations are always equally upright. One always wants one's good, but one does not always see it: one can never corrupt the people, but one can often cause it to be mistaken, and only when it is, does it appear to want what is bad.

There is often a considerable difference between the will of all and the general will: the latter looks only to the common interest, the former looks to private interest, and is nothing but a sum of particular wills. . . .

Of the Limits of Sovereign Power

. . . Just as nature gives each man absolute power over his members, the social pact gives the body politic absolute power over all of its members, and it is this same power which, directed by the general will, bears, as I have said, the name of sovereignty. . . .

It is agreed that each man alienates by the social pact only that portion of his power, his goods, his freedom, which it is important for the community to be able to use, but it should also be agreed to that the Sovereign is alone judge of that importance. . . .

. . . The social pact establishes among the Citizens an equality such that all commit themselves under the same conditions and must all enjoy the same rights. Thus by the nature of the pact every act of sovereignty, that is to say every genuine act of the general will, either obligates or favors all Citizens equally.

7

MAXIMILIEN ROBESPIERRE

Eulogies to Rousseau

1790s

Maximilien Robespierre (1758–1794) was a French lawyer and politician who became one of the most powerful leaders of the French Revolution. Known as "the Incorruptible" because of his ascetic dedication to his moral principles, he dominated the Committee of Public Safety, which effectively ruled France during the Revolution's most bloody phase, the Reign of Terror. During this period (June 1793–July 1794), thousands of French men and women were imprisoned or executed for opposing the Revolution. In these two excerpts—one from a speech delivered by Robespierre at the National Convention, the other from a draft found among his private papers—Robespierre expresses his almost religious reverence for Jean-Jacques Rousseau.

[From *Le Moniteur Universel*, May 8, 1794]
For a long time, enlightened observers could perceive some of the symptoms of the present revolution. All important events were tending

From *Réimpression de l'Ancien Moniteur, Seule Histoire Authentique et Inalterée de la Révolution Française* (Paris: Henri Plon, 1861), 20:408; and from "Dédicace à Jean-Jacques Rousseau," *Œuvres complètes de Maximilien Robespierre*, ed. Victor Barbier and Charles Vellay (Paris: Bureau de la Revue historique de la Révolution française, 1910–1913), I:212. Translated by Helena Rosenblatt.

toward it. . . . Famous men of letters, because of their influence on opinion, began to have influence on the affairs of state. . . . These prima donnas sometimes denounced despotism in public, and yet they accepted pensions from despots; they wrote books against the court, and dedications to kings. . . . They were proud in their writings and grovelling in the antechambers. . . . We owe in large part to them that sort of practical philosophy which, reducing selfishness to a system, sees human society as a war of stratagems . . . and the world as the patrimony of clever egoists.

Among those, in the period of which I speak, who distinguished themselves in the career of letters and philosophy, one man, by the elevation of his soul and the grandeur of his character, showed himself worthy of the position of teacher of the human race. . . . The purity of his doctrine, drawn from nature and from a profound hatred of vice, as much as his invincible disdain for intriguing sophists[10] who usurped the name *philosophe*, brought upon him the hatred and persecution of his rivals and false friends. Ah! If he had witnessed this revolution of which he was the precursor, and which brought him to the Pantheon, who can doubt that his generous soul would have embraced with rapture the cause of justice and equality!

[From Robespierre's private papers]
Citizen of Geneva! . . . Divine man, you have taught me to know myself. . . . You made me appreciate the dignity of my nature and reflect on the great principles of the social order. . . . Called to play a role in the midst of the greatest events which have ever shaken the world, assisting in the agony of despotism and the revival of true sovereignty . . . I want to follow your venerated path . . . happy if . . . I remain constantly faithful to the inspiration which I have drawn from your writings.

---

[10] Originally a certain class of ancient Greek philosopher, *sophist* later came to mean anyone who reasons in a superficial, subtle, and fundamentally unsound way.

8

BENJAMIN CONSTANT

The Principles of Politics

1810

Born in Lausanne, Switzerland, Benjamin Constant (1767–1830) was one of the most important political thinkers of the early nineteenth century and a founding father of modern liberalism. Profoundly affected by the French Revolution, he blamed its derailment into the Reign of Terror on those who espoused certain "Rousseauean" ideas. This excerpt shows Constant to be both an admirer and a critic of Rousseau's political philosophy. Constant saw the dangers lurking in some of Rousseau's principles and sought to warn people against them.

The Consequences of Rousseau's Theory

When you have affirmed on principle the view that the prerogatives of society always become, finally, those of government, you understand immediately how necessary it is that political power be limited. If it is not, individual existence is on the one hand subjected without qualification to the general will, while on the other, the general will finds itself represented without appeal by the will of the governors. These representatives of the general will have powers all the more formidable in that they call themselves mere pliant instruments of this alleged will and possess the means of enforcement or enticement necessary to ensure that it is manifested in ways which suit them. What no tyrant would dare to do in his own name, the latter legitimate by the unlimited extension of boundless political authority. They seek the enlargement of the powers they need, from the very owner of political authority, that is, the people, whose omnipotence is there only to justify their encroachments. The most unjust laws and oppressive institutions are obligatory, as the expression of the general will. For individuals, says Rousseau, having

From Benjamin Constant, *Principles of Politics Applicable to All Governments*, ed. Etienne Hofmann, trans. Dennis O'Keeffe (Indianapolis: Liberty Fund, 2003), 19–20, 25–26. Originally published in French as Etienne Hofmann, ed., *Les "Principes de politique" de Benjamin Constant: La genèse d'une oeuvre et l'évolution de la pensée de leur auteur (1789–1806)* (Geneva: Librairie Droz, 1980).

alienated their all to the benefit of the collectivity, can have no will other than that general will. Obeying this, they obey only themselves, and are all the freer the more implicitly they obey.

. . . When no limit to political authority is acknowledged, the people's leaders, in a popular government, are not defenders of freedom, but aspiring tyrants. . . . When it has a representative constitution, a nation is free only when its delegates are held in check. It would be easy to show, by means of countless examples, that the gross sophisms of the most ardent apostles of the Terror, in the most revolting circumstances, were only perfectly consistent consequences of Rousseau's principles. . . .

I do not side at all with [Rousseau's] detractors. A rabble of inferior minds, who see their brief success as consisting in calling into doubt every redoubtable truth, is excitedly anxious to take away his greatness. This is just one more reason to render him our homage. He was the first writer to popularize the sense of our rights. His was a voice to stir generous hearts and independent spirits. But what he felt so powerfully, he did not know how to define precisely. . . . What is meant by rights which one enjoys all the more for having given them away completely? Just what is a freedom in virtue of which one is all the more free the more unquestioningly one does what runs counter to one's own wishes? These are deadly theological sophisms such as give weapons to all tyrannies, to the tyranny of one man, to that of a few people, to the legally constituted kind, and to the kind dominated by popular fury! Jean-Jacques's errors have seduced many friends of freedom, because they were established to counter other, more degrading mistakes. Even so, we cannot refute them strongly enough, because they put insuperable obstacles in the way of any free or moderate constitution, and they supply a banal pretext for all manner of political outrages.

A Jean-Jacques Rousseau Chronology
(1712–1794)

1712 Jean-Jacques Rousseau is born in Geneva on June 28 to Isaac Rousseau, a watchmaker, and Suzanne Bernard Rousseau. His mother dies shortly after his birth.

1728 Rousseau leaves Geneva at the age of sixteen and converts to Catholicism, thereby forfeiting his Genevan citizenship.

1742 Arrives in Paris and joins the world of the *philosophes*.

1749 Denis Diderot is thrown into prison. While walking to visit him, Rousseau reads about an essay competition given by the Academy of Dijon and experiences his "Illumination at Vincennes."

1750 Rousseau submits *Discourse on the Sciences and Arts* to the Academy of Dijon, which awards him first prize.

1753 Another essay competition provokes Rousseau to write the *Discourse on the Origin and Foundations of Inequality among Men*. It does not win a prize and is not well received.

1754 Rousseau returns to Geneva, reconverts to Protestantism, and regains his citizenship.

1755 Publishes the *Discourse on the Origin and Foundations of Inequality among Men* with a *Dedication to Geneva*. Neither text is well received.

1756 To the disappointment of his Parisian friends, Rousseau withdraws to a cottage outside the city where he can work in relative solitude.

1758 Rousseau publishes *Letter to d'Alembert*, which completes his break with the *philosophes*.

1761 Publishes his novel, *Julie, or the New Heloise*, which is hugely successful. A cult begins to grow around him.

1762 Publishes *The Social Contract* (May 15) and *Emile* (May 22). Both are declared subversive by the French and Genevan authorities, and warrants are issued for Rousseau's arrest, forcing him to live as an exile and fugitive from justice for eight years. Increasingly, he feels betrayed, persecuted, and misunderstood.

1764 Rousseau renounces his Genevan citizenship.

1765 Decides to write an autobiography, which becomes the *Confessions.*

1770 Is allowed to return to Paris, where he lives a quiet life.

1778 Rousseau dies suddenly on July 2.

1789 The French Revolution begins.

1794 Rousseau's ashes are transferred to the Panthéon in Paris, where he is buried next to other "national heroes."

Questions for Consideration

1. Compare and contrast Rousseau's view of the state of nature with those of Bossuet, Hobbes, Pufendorf, and Locke.
2. How many "steps to society" are there in the Second Discourse? Describe each stage and how it gives way to the next.
3. What do you think Rousseau meant by "perfectibility"?
4. How does Rousseau explain the difference between *amour propre* and *amour de soi-même*?
5. Describe Rousseau's views on the origin of language.
6. How does Rousseau's view of property differ from Locke's? What do you think might have caused their different perspectives? Which view is more relevant today?
7. It has been said that Rousseau held paradoxical views on gender. Compare his treatment of women in the Dedication to that in the Second Discourse itself. Do you think his positions in the two texts are reconcilable?
8. Like Locke (see Note XII) and Buffon (Document 5), Rousseau spends a good deal of time comparing human beings to animals. How is Rousseau's description of a human being different from Locke's and Buffon's?
9. Based on what he wrote in the Second Discourse, some people say that Rousseau was an optimist about human nature, while others say he was a pessimist. Which view do you think is correct?
10. Robespierre (Document 7) drew inspiration from Rousseau, while Constant (Document 8) believed his theories to be dangerous. On the basis of your own reading of the Second Discourse and the excerpts from *The Social Contract*, assess the claim of those who see a potential for terror and tyranny in Rousseau's thought.
11. How do you think Rousseau's life contributed to his political philosophy?
12. It is said that what makes a text truly great is its ability to remain relevant beyond its own time period. What lessons in the Second Discourse do you think are still meaningful today?

13. In the Dedication, Rousseau refers to something he calls "democratic government." Drawing also upon what he says in the Second Discourse and in *The Social Contract*, what do you think Rousseau means by this?

14. In Note IX, Rousseau refers to "the secret aspirations of the heart of every civilized man." What do you think he is alluding to? How do the aspirations of civilized man compare to those of natural man?

Selected Bibliography

AUTHORITATIVE EDITIONS

Rousseau, Jean-Jacques. *The Collected Writings of Rousseau.* Edited by Roger D. Masters and Christopher Kelly. 9 vols. Hanover, N.H.: University Press of New England, 1990–2010.
————. *Œuvres complètes.* Edited by Bernard Gagnebin and Marcel Raymond. 5 vols. Paris: Bibliothèque de la Pléiade, 1959–1995.

BIOGRAPHIES

Cranston, Maurice. *Jean-Jacques: The Early Life and Work of Jean-Jacques Rousseau, 1712–1754.* London: Allan Lane, 1983.
————. *The Noble Savage: Jean-Jacques Rousseau, 1754–1762.* London: Allan Lane, 1991.
————. *The Solitary Self: Jean-Jacques Rousseau in Exile and Adversity.* Chicago: University of Chicago Press, 1997.
Guéhenno, Jean. *Jean-Jacques Rousseau.* Translated by John and Doreen Weightman. London: Routledge, 1967.

GENERAL STUDIES OF ROUSSEAU'S THOUGHT

Dent, N. J. H. *A Rousseau Dictionary.* Oxford, U.K.: Blackwell, 1992.
Hendel, C. W. *Jean-Jacques Rousseau: Moralist,* 2nd ed. Indianapolis, Ind.: Oxford University Press, 1962.
Masters, Roger. *The Political Philosophy of Rousseau.* Princeton, N.J.: Princeton University Press, 1968.
Melzer, Arthur. *The Natural Goodness of Man: On the System of Rousseau's Thought.* Chicago: University of Chicago Press, 1990.
Miller, James. *Rousseau: Dreamer of Democracy.* New Haven, Conn.: Yale University Press, 1984.
O'Hagan, Timothy. *Rousseau.* New York: Routledge, 2003.
Orwin, Clifford, and Nathan Tarcov, eds. *The Legacy of Rousseau.* Chicago: University of Chicago Press, 1997.
Rosenblatt, Helena. *Rousseau and Geneva: From the First Discourse to the Social Contract, 1749–1762.* Cambridge, U.K.: Cambridge University Press, 1997.

Shklar, Judith. *Men and Citizens: A Study of Rousseau's Social Theory*, 2nd ed. Cambridge, U.K.: Cambridge University Press, 1985.

Starobinski, Jean. *Jean-Jacques Rousseau: Transparency and Obstruction*. Translated by Arthur Goldhammer. Chicago: University of Chicago Press, 1988.

Wokler, Robert. *Rousseau*. Oxford, U.K.: Oxford University Press, 1995.

ROUSSEAU'S STATE OF NATURE

Gourevitch, Victor. "Rousseau's Pure State of Nature." *Interpretation* 16 (1988): 23–59.

Horowitz, Asher. *Rousseau, Nature, and History*. Toronto: University of Toronto Press, 1986.

Lane, Joseph, and Rebecca Clark. "The Solitary Walker in the Political World: The Paradoxes of Rousseau and Deep Ecology." *Political Theory* 34, no. 1 (February 2006): 62–94.

Lovejoy, Arthur. "The Supposed Primitivism of Rousseau's Discourse on Inequality." *Essays in the History of Ideas*. Baltimore: Johns Hopkins University Press, 1948.

Moran, Francis, III. "Between Primates and Primitives: Natural Man as the Missing Link in Rousseau's Second Discourse." *Journal of the History of Ideas* 54 (January 1993): 37–58.

Wokler, Robert. "Anthropology and Conjectural History in the Enlightenment." In *Inventing Human Science: Eighteenth-Century Domains*, edited by Christopher Fox, Roy Porter, and Robert Wokler, 31–52. Berkeley: University of California Press, 1995.

ROUSSEAU AND GENDER

Steinbrügge, Lieselotte. *The Moral Sex: Woman's Nature in the French Enlightenment*. Translated by Pamela Selwyn. New York: Oxford University Press, 1995.

Thomas, Paul. "Jean-Jacques Rousseau, Sexist?" In "Constructing Gender Difference: The French Tradition," special issue, *Feminist Studies* 17, no. 2 (Summer 1991): 195–217.

Weiss, Penny, and Anne Harper. "Rousseau's Political Defense of the Sex-Roled Family." *Hypatia* 5, no. 3 (Autumn 1990): 90–105.

ROUSSEAU AND THE FRENCH REVOLUTION

Blum, Carol. *Rousseau and the Republic of Virtue: The Language of Politics in the French Revolution*. Ithaca, N.Y.: Cornell University Press, 1986.

Furet, François. "Rousseau and the French Revolution." In *The Legacy of Rousseau*, edited by Clifford Orwin and Nathan Tarcov, 168–82. Chicago: University of Chicago Press, 1997.

McDonald, Joan. *Rousseau and the French Revolution, 1762–1791*. London: Athlone Press, 1965.

McNeil, Gordon. "The Cult of Rousseau and the French Revolution." *Journal of the History of Ideas* 6, no. 2 (April 1945): 197–212.

Swenson, James. *On Jean-Jacques Rousseau: Considered as One of the First Authors of the Revolution*. Stanford, Calif.: Stanford University Press, 2000.

Acknowledgments (continued from p. iv)

Document 1: From Jacques-Bénigne Bossuet, *Politics Drawn from the Very Words of Holy Scripture*, ed and trans. Patrick Riley (Cambridge, U.K.: Cambridge University Press, 1999). Reprinted with the permission of Cambridge University Press.

Document 3: From Samuel Pufendorf, *On the Duty of Man and Citizen*, ed. James Tully, trans. Michael Silverthorne (Cambridge, U.K.: Cambridge University Press, 2000). Reprinted with the permission of Cambridge University Press.

Document 6: From Jean-Jacques Rousseau, *Of the Social Contract or Principles of Political Right*, in *The Social Contract and Other Later Political Writings*, ed. and trans. Victor Gourevitch (Cambridge, U.K.: Cambridge University Press, 1997). Reprinted with the permission of Cambridge University Press.

Document 8: From Benjamin Constant, *Principles of Politics Applicable to All Governments*, ed. Etienne Hofmann, trans. Dennis O'Keeffe (Indianapolis: Liberty Fund, 2003), 19–20, 25–26. Reprinted with the permission of the Liberty Fund and Librairie Droz.

Index

abilities and circumstances of man, 11, 14, 36, 47, 50, 52–53, 57, 61–62
absolute monarchy
  civil society, and role of, 43
  criticism of, 147–48
  divine right of kings and, 7–8, 88, 95, 129–32
  France and, 2, 7, 18, 22, 86
  laws formed after period of, 85–87, 89–90
  man's need for, 8–9, 87, 133–34, 136–37
  revolutions to overthrow governments preceded by, 93
  rights of man and, 87–88
  Social Contract, The (Rousseau) and, 142–43
Academy of Dijon, 5, 6, 10, 149
agriculture/farming, 12, 54, 77–78, 92, 107–8
Allegory of the Revolution (Jeaurat de Bertry), 21*f*
amour de soi-même (self-preservation). *See* self-preservation (*amour de soi-même*)
amour propre (artificial/relative sentiment)
  definition of, ix, 122
  pity, and balance with, 75–76
  pride in civil society and, 14–16, 43, 71, 103, 104
  reason and, 63, 78
  self-preservation, and balance with, 61–62
  See also passions
anatomy, and animals compared with natural man, 45
animals
  knowledge of man compared with instincts of, 96
  natural law and, 38–39
  natural man compared with anthropomorphic, 110–14
  natural man's superiority compared with inferiority of, 139–40
  nature, and competition between natural man and, 70–71
  skills of natural man compared with attacks by, 47–48
  See also animals compared with natural man
animals compared with natural man
  anatomy, 45
  conflicts/warfare, 46–47, 99–100, 102, 104–5, 107, 111, 117–18, 121–22

diet, 46, 99–100, 102
family associations, 50, 118–19
freedom, 14, 85
language/communication, 58, 121
longevity, 102
love relationships, 65–66, 140
perfectibility, 51–52, 58, 107, 110, 112–13
pity, 62, 122
procreation, 66
strength, 45, 46
walking habits, 97–98
See also animals
anthropomorphic animals, 110–14
Aristotle, 27, 37, 45
artificial/relative sentiment (*amour propre*). *See amour propre* (artificial/relative sentiment); passions
arts and sciences, 6, 54, 103, 107, 108

Barbeyrac, Jean, 8, 86
Bossuet, Jacques-Bénigne
  Politics Drawn from the Very Words of Holy Scripture, 7, 129–32
Buffon, George-Louis Leclerc de
  Discourse on the Nature of Animals, 139–40
  longevity of animals compared with man's and, 102
  love relationships and, 140
  man's nobility and, 140
  Natural History, 15, 25*n*22, 98–99
Burlamaqui, Jean-Jacques, 8, 38

Catholicism, 3, 18, 149
celebrations and dancing, in leisure time, 74–76
Chardin, Jean, 115
childhood, of natural man, 48, 102
circumstances and abilities of man, 11, 14, 36, 47, 50, 52–53, 57, 61–62
civil/political rights. *See* rights of man
civil society
  absolute monarchy and, 43
  arts and sciences in, 54, 103, 107, 108
  equality in, 17–18, 145
  freedom versus dependency in, 29, 68
  God's role in, 40, 43, 60

157